NEW ORLEANS
ON THE HALF-SHELL

NEW ORLEANS
ON THE HALF-SHELL

A NATIVE'S GUIDE
TO THE CRESCENT CITY

Alan Graham
James Taylor

PELICAN PUBLISHING COMPANY
GRETNA 1996

First published by New Bohemian Press, 1981

First edition, 1981
First Pelican printing, 1981
Third printing, 1984
Second edition, 1990
Third edition, 1996

*The word "Pelican" and the depiction of a pelican are trademarks
of Pelican Publishing Company, Inc., and are registered
in the U.S. Patent and Trademark Office.*

Information in this guidebook is based on authoritative data available at the
time of printing and is subject to change without notice. Readers are asked
to take this into account when consulting this guide.

Library of Congress Cataloging-in-Publication Data

Graham, Alan, 1950-
  New Orleans on the half-shell : a native's guide to the Crescent
City / Alan Graham, James Taylor. — 3rd ed.
    p. cm.
  Graham's name appears first on the previous edition.
  ISBN 1-56554-058-1 (pb)
  1. New Orleans (La.)—Guidebooks.   I. Taylor, James, 1949- .
II. Title.
F379.N53T38   1996
917.63'350463—dc20   94-42798
                                                                                         CIP

Cover design by Carol Lasky Studios, Boston
Art by Jeff Jennings

Manufactured in the United States of America
Published by Pelican Publishing Company, Inc.
1101 Monroe Street, Gretna, Louisiana 70053

For Heather Moreau,
Anglo-French Canadian jewel,
lover of New Orleans,
who swept a native heart,
in the nick of time.
                    —A. G.

To Dottie, my wife,
and to my children:
Jameson and Mallory.
                    —J. T.

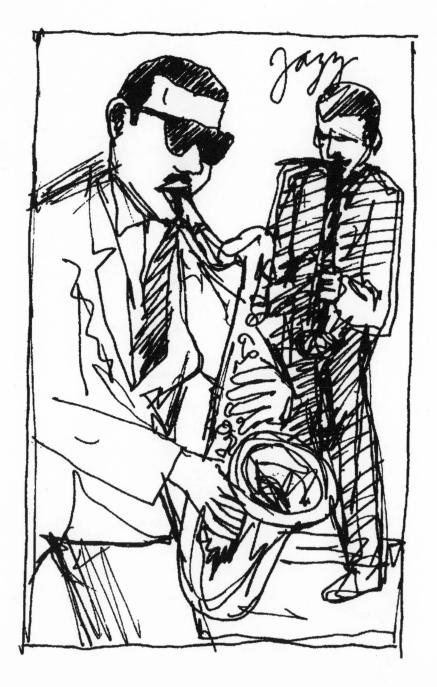

Contents

PREFACE 9

ACKNOWLEDGMENTS 11

Half-Shell Awards..12

Where Yat! 15

Survival 17

Directory 29

The Lay of the Land 31

Getting Around..33

Food..41

Music and Night Life..71

Drinking Establishments 93

Civilized Pleasures 97

Mardi Gras 99

Jazz Fest 105

Other Fairs and Festivals 109

New Orleans Medley 113

Political Realities..117

The Arts..119

Films in New Orleans 133

Recreation..141

Spectator Sports..155

Tours..159

Free and Cheap Things to Do with Kids 163

Yat Vernacular 169
Creole or Cajun—A World of Difference!? 173
The Authors 175

Preface

Sometime around spring 1979, Alan Graham went to Stockholm and tired quickly of the Frommer and Fielding guidebooks to that glorious city. He picked up a pamphlet called the "All-Ternative Guide to Stockholm." When he returned to New Orleans, he toyed with a new idea, a concept for an informative, witty, and irreverent guide to our city. He showed me the Swedish guide and announced that he was going to write a "native's" guide to New Orleans for people who weren't going to Antoine's, staying at the Royal Orleans—in short, a book for the budget conscious with a splurge or two. A few months later, he still wanted to write the guide but also wanted a coauthor for the project. He asked if I was interested and the rest is history. We took up residence at Alan's Pontchartrain Boulevard dining-room table for six weeks or so while we brainstormed, schemed, organized, and wrote about every restaurant, bar and musical group, peculiarity, and oddity that we knew about New Orleans—in long hand.

We were both teaching high school at the time, so the next step was to borrow typewriters from our schools, a regular one for the primary text and one with a script font for the "lagniappe" boxes. You guessed it—we were embarking on the self-publishing journey. Alan typed because he was faster. We did the layout and design, if you can truly say it was designed. Nonetheless, he typed with the margins set to page width and I pasted the text and pictures. The pictures were drawn by Sheila Cardona and Donna Barry, friends upon whom we imposed, Huan Hoang, a student, and myself in a desperate, last-minute attempt to fill some space. (The smiling shrimp returns in this edition.) To do the titles, we knew enough to go to an art-supply store and get some

press on letters. We just didn't know how to transfer them to the page. We were amateurs, but fast-learning amateurs.

The first edition sold for three dollars and all our friends and relatives probably still have several copies. We pounded the pavement and put them in several bookstores on consignment. I still recall the thrill when Sidney Pampo at Sidney's Newsstand on Decatur Street took ten copies and paid cash on the spot.

Copies were sent to reviewers and gossip columnists all over town. The book reviewer at *The Times-Picayune*, the late Mabel Simmons, felt this pathetic little pamphlet had some merit and gave it a most enthusiastic thumbs up. Other scribes wrote kindly as well.

At the time, Alan was teaching on the West Bank. One day on his way home from work, he stopped in at the Gretna offices of Pelican Publishing Company. He boldly approached the secretary and asked to see the editor. He was politely advised not to let the door hit him on his way out. Undaunted, he brought forth the little homemade book along with our "clippings." The secretary relented.

The editor at the time was an unusually wise woman named Frumie Selchen. Frumie, who later left publishing to tend an organic farm in New Hampshire, was sympathetic to our "underground" guide. She somehow convinced Milburn Calhoun, the publisher, to sign us—and the rest is history, as they say. *Half-Shell* continued in its homemade format until 1990, when it became a "real book." An entirely new text was complemented with new art by Jeff Jennings and the current cover by Carol Lasky.

As we approach the end of the millennium, we bring you yet another edition. New Orleans is on the verge of what feels to be a transformation of unprecedented proportion. We celebrate our past and anticipate the future. Regardless of the magnitude of the changes that are certain to occur, when the next edition of *Half-Shell* rolls around we can guarantee you that you will still be able to get a great "erster po' boy" at Uglesich's and a chili and cheese omelet at Camellia Grill. We'll be here to tell you about them and much more. Stay tuned.

Acknowledgments

Following a several-year stay during the seventies, Carol Lasky could not shake the mysterious allure that characterizes New Orleans. From the environs of her studio in Boston, Carol successfully conjured up this state-of-the-art cover design, which the authors embraced immediately. She even selected a typeface for the title called "Fat Louis," which defines the funkiness of *Half-Shell*.

The authors and Carol all worked together in 1972 and 1973 at a famous New Orleans train-station restaurant. Carol now designs magazine and book covers and engages in other artistic endeavors at Carol Lasky Studios in Boston. We thank her for her sensational contribution to our book. It was great to work together again. Draggin' a mush!

Jeff Jennings, who did the interior artwork for this book, spent his childhood in Belfast, Maine. He attended art school in Portland, Oreg., where he received his bachelor of fine arts degree. He spent the next ten years working as an artist and boatbuilder. He now resides in New Orleans and completed study at the University of New Orleans Graduate School of Fine Arts. Jeff is married to Maureen Blackburn and has a daughter, Madeleine.

Half-Shell Awards

No boring bean awards, no snotty little stars and a half—we're talking hard-to-get Half-Shell Awards. Throughout this edition of *Half-Shell* you will find the introduction of the Half-Shell Award, bestowed to recognize excellence. We give these awards stingily and not just for food.

To receive an award the nominee must meet one or more of our stringent criteria:

1. Extraordinary performance.

2. Contribution or value.

3. Quality.

4. AJ Preference Formula (because Alan and Jim say so).

Yeah, you right. There's nothing finer than an oyster award: succulent, seductive, and salty. They taste great and are only beautiful when you hold them sideways. We decided to fill those shells in honor of our 15th year and brand-new edition.

NEW ORLEANS
ON THE HALF-SHELL

Where Yat!

Where yat, indeed! You're in New Orleans, of course: 29°56' latitude, 90°04' longitude, and one treacherous foot below sea level; the Big Easy, the City That Care Forgot, and all that jazz that's become cliché for newspaper headlines and chamber of commerce brochures. You've finally fulfilled that lifelong ambition to get to the French Quarter, Mardi Gras, or Jazz Fest. What do you do after you've walked down Bourbon Street and seen Jackson Square? If you want to see the glossy tourist haven of picture-postcard fame, take a tour on one of those big air-conditioned buses. If you want to experience the city as only the natives know it, read this book! We want to show you how to stay here and enjoy the best that New Orleans has to offer, without depleting the trust fund.

New Orleanians are very chauvinistic. We believe this is the best city in the galaxy. We're certain that if you follow our recommendations, even the hard-core skeptics will be convinced. And as for this "where yat" business . . . well, we'll get to that.

LAGNIAPPE

Lagniappe is a French word that means "something extra." Many lagniappe boxes are scattered throughout this book, consisting of highlights that are of special interest to visitors and natives alike.

Survival

Ordinances in New Orleans may be referred to as the "sometimes" ordinances—sometimes they're enforced and sometimes they're not. There are many variables to consider that could comprise an entire book in and of themselves. Regardless of degree of enforcement, there are some things you need to know in order to have a hassle-free visit.

Places to Avoid

Like other American urban areas, New Orleans is not exempt from crime. Common sense should dictate procedures in the city, but here are some basic rules to follow and areas to avoid.

1. Do not stray from the beaten path. To either side is the swamp. The swamp is full of vipers. Be careful.
2. Use caution when venturing into public rest rooms alone, especially at night at the French Market.
3. Avoid the following: the historic New Orleans cemeteries, unless you are in a large group.

CEMETERIES

Being below sea level, New Orleans buries her dead in aboveground vaults so the bodies will not float away. These cemeteries are very interesting and picturesque. The oldest cemeteries are located at the back of the French Quarter near Claiborne Avenue and can be seen from Interstate 10. This is the location of the tomb of the famous voodoo queen, Marie Laveau. (Caution: These cemeteries are also havens for muggers. If you visit, be careful— you don't want to become a permanent resident.)

17

4. The wharf and dock area along the river, including the Moonwalk at night.

5. All parks after sunset.

6. The Garden District has beautiful mansions to view, but when dusk arrives it is time to depart; the mansions become fortresses and you become a target.

7. Just remember that any place that doesn't look safe usually isn't!

8. If you have an out-of-state driver's license and plate, be especially careful not to violate traffic laws. If you are from a state without a reciprocity agreement with Louisiana (and who really knows for sure?), your license will be confiscated after such a violation. If you are from out of state and don't have your license in your possession when you get stopped in your car, you will go to jail. You will be strip searched, deloused, and locked up. You will not be a good P.R. person for New Orleans. Think about it.

Driving in New Orleans

We have a couple of words of wisdom: drive defensively. New Orleans drivers are among the worst anywhere. A green light means go, a yellow light means go faster, and a red light means the third car to reach the intersection might stop. Keep an eye out—seriously.

Speed Kills (and Can Also Be Quite Expensive)

The speed limit on undivided streets is 25 mph, and on the divided avenues such as St. Charles, Canal, and Carrollton it is 35. Aside from the obvious safety considerations, a speeding ticket for going 10 miles an hour over the limit will cost you over a hundred dollars. If you're from out of town, you may be taken to jail to pay right then, or to visit until you do pay. The other danger is to your car. If you hit one of the many massive street craters at 45 miles an hour, you can blow a tire, bend a rim, or at the very least, knock your front end out of alignment. In the worst-case scenario, major front-end damage can result. We are, after all, below sea level and sinking potholes abound.

Parking

There are three rules that must be followed when parking downtown: read the signs, read the signs, and, most importantly, read the signs. Parking regulations are enforced with great vigor. Although parking tickets are an aggravation, the more serious threats to a visitor's attitude and pocket book are the tow trucks, which circle the city like hungry vultures. One hint of carelessness from an unsuspecting driver and, depending on the particular sign one may have ignored, they descend.

The discovery that one's car is not still parked in the spot where it was left will send the unfortunate owner through a host of conflicting emotions. Is it lost, stolen, maybe on the next corner? The relief you'll experience when you discover that it's only in the auto pound will turn immediately into anger and frustration when you're faced with the hundred-dollar-plus fine you will have to pay on the spot (credit cards accepted). Parking meters are enforced Monday through Friday during business hours (8-6). Feed them.

Car Accidents

All traffic accidents should be reported to the New Orleans Police Department (821-2222). However, if yours is of a minor nature, i.e., no injuries (and we hope that if you have an accident it is minor), expect a long wait for the authorities. In the interim, exchange the necessary information, and then make yourself comfortable. If you're a reader, we recommend *War and Peace*; you'll be there a while.

Dangerous Intersections

Be exceptionally aware of Canal Street at Claiborne, St. Charles at Carrollton, and Veterans at Causeway. And by all means, if you are headed for the fairgrounds look out for the intersection of Gentilly Boulevard, St. Bernard Avenue, and Desaix Boulevard. This is worse than the Champs-Elysées in Paris: there are 21 lights at this complex, nightmare intersection.

Litterbugs

Give the city a break! Native New Orleanians are infamous for trash pollution and the city's environment is dirty enough. In addition, local litter laws are being strictly enforced and a heavy fine might result. There are rumors of litter vigilantes out there. Play it safe; put it in the can.

Drinking

The local saying "if you're tall enough to see over the bar, then you're of drinking age" is basically true, though somewhat exaggerated. Drinking laws are among the most liberal in the country:

1. In the wild and wooly days (pre-1986), one only had to appear to be 18 in order to purchase liquor or be admitted to bars. Now, in these days of responsible consumption, the government has decreed that drinkers must be 21 or it will disperse no highway funds to the states. Louisiana resisted this mandate briefly, but finally succumbed to fiscal sanity. Now one must appear to be 21.

USELESS FACTS

Population: *just over fi million*
            Greater N.O.: 1 million
            French Quarter: 6,000

Official languages: *English, Spanish, French, and Yat*

Flags: *France, Spain, Confederacy, U.S., Mardi Gras*

Industries: *tourism, foreign trade*

Altitude: *just below sea level and sinking*

2. All bars, grocery stores, and convenience stores may sell beer, wine, and liquor 24 hours a day, 7 days a week, 365 days a year, including Sundays, holidays, and election day.

3. Bars may serve alcohol at any hour; there are no time restrictions.

4. You are allowed to drink on the streets of New Orleans, but your beverage cannot be in a bottle or can unless it is in a protective container. Try to use plastic or paper cups.

5. Even though New Orleans has a reputation as a hard-drinking party town, we would hope that no one has to tell you not to drink and drive. Designate a driver, take a cab, or ride the buses and streetcars. You can imagine the expense and inconvenience of a driving-while-intoxicated charge. You *will* go to jail.

6. The number for Alcoholics Anonymous is 525-1178.

Twenty-four Hours

New Orleans is a round-the-clock town. The inducement of having places to go at all hours often entices visitors and locals alike to embark on all-night excursions into Never Never Land. If you find yourself on one of these outings and in need of towing service or a bite to eat at 4 A.M., what should you do? Perhaps this list can help. Some of these listings can be found under other headings, but are included here for easy reference.

DRUGSTORES AND PRESCRIPTIONS

Eckerd's 3400 Canal St. (488-6661)

K&B 3100 Gentilly Blvd. at Elysian Fields (947-6611)

   3401 St. Charles Ave. (895-0344) (also, several in Metairie)

Walgreen's 3311 Canal St. (822-8070)

WRECKER SERVICE

City Park Shell 3494 Esplanade Ave. (488-1720)

Dan Usner Shell 6201 S. Claiborne Ave. (across from Tulane University) (866-2762)

Lee White Wrecker Service 2111 22nd St., Kenner (466-1978)

DOUGHNUTS

Cafe du Monde French Market, across from Jackson Square in the Quarter (561-9235) Always highly recommended.

Morning Call 3325 Severn in Metairie, across from Lakeside Shopping Center (888-4068) Highly recommended even if they did move to Main Street Metry.

Dunkin' Donuts 4015 Veterans Hwy. (887-3051)

Tastee Donuts They're everywhere! They're everywhere! Check the Yellow Pages under *Doughnuts*. We do recommend No. 58 at 3401 Prytania because that's where you'll find one of our great R&B songwriters, Earl ("Trick Bag") King. The cover for his album *Glaze* was shot there.

RESTAURANTS

Mardi Gras Truck Stop 2401 Elysian Fields Ave. (945-1000)

Hummingbird Grill 804 St. Charles Ave. (561-9229)

St. Charles Tavern 1433 St. Charles Ave. (523-9823)

Igor's Lounge and Game Room 2133 St. Charles Ave. (522-2145)

Clover Grill Bourbon and Dumaine (523-0904)

Bailey's Restaurant Baronne near Canal (in the Fairmont Hotel) (529-7111)

Gendusa Bakery 1801 N. Rampart (945-5817)

CAFE AU LAIT AND BEIGNETS

An old Louisiana custom is drinking a cup of coffee and chicory with hot milk along with warm, square, hole-less, powdered-sugar-covered doughnuts. Try the outdoor Cafe du Monde by Jackson Square for a budget breakfast or evening delight.

La Peniche 1940 Dauphine (943-1460)
Quarter Scene 900 Dumaine (522-6533)
Denny's Restaurants (a chain restaurant, but open 24 hours nevertheless)

5769 Crowder Blvd. (246-3600)

3116 S. I-10 Service Rd., Metairie (837-2290)

5910 Veterans Hwy. (where I-10 crosses Vets) (887-8007)

BARS

Come on, give us a break! If you can't find a 24-hour bar, then you're not in New Orleans. But try the French Quarter, especially the Old Absinthe Bar at 400 Bourbon, if you want ambience and relative safety at 5 A.M.

Sleeping

New Orleans has many expensive hotels. These are located primarily in the French Quarter and Central Business District. The ultra-expensive tourist season is September through May. In the summer months the prices moderate somewhat, and a few hotels offer package rates. Unless you're traveling on an expense account or Daddy's money, a short stay puts a big hole in the travel budget.

For a taste of the elegance and tradition of a bygone era, there is a multitude of small hotels and guesthouses in the French Quarter and Uptown areas. Most are furnished with antiques, and some have patios and courtyards that are both intimate and charming. Many are as expensive as the large hotels.

The best lodging deal in town is the bed and breakfast. Prices begin at under $50 and escalate into the $100 range, but the price is not the best part of the deal. These establishments are usually the homes of empty nesters or couples who have renovated one of our large, often historic, buildings. The environs are typical of our way of life here at sea level.

There is an added benefit if good value and ambience aren't enough for you. Often, the proprietors add a little lagniappe. One home we know of has a harp room and the hostess entertains her guests in the afternoon. Another host is a history buff who takes his visitors on walking tours of the neighborhood. The whole affair is so much more personal than a stay in one of those high-rise hotels downtown.

Some of the B&Bs are listed in the Yellow Pages, but the best way to ensure a first-class establishment is to reserve your accommodations through a booking service. These services inspect their establishments on a regular basis and can give you a variety of options.

Bed and Breakfast, Inc. (488-4640)

New Orleans Bed and Breakfast Reservation Service (838-0071)

RECOMMENDED B&BS IN UNCOMMON ENVIRONS

While bed and breakfast inns seem to be concentrated in the French Quarter, there are better budget deals to be had in other charming neighborhoods and historic areas. They are also accessible to other parts of the city, including the French Quarter. We want to highly recommend three that we have selected for reasons that will become obvious as you read further.

The Duvigneaud House and the Degas House are two wonderful examples of neighborhood preservation, culture, history, and restoration that define the richness of many parts of our city. Both are situated in the fabulous Faubourg St. John area around Bayou St. John, City Park, and Esplanade Avenue. While probably the most scenic area of the city, it is often overlooked by visitors, newcomers, and natives alike due to the emphasis placed upon Uptown St. Charles Avenue, with its quaint streetcar line and historic homes, and of course, our major attraction, the French Quarter. Deserving as they are of all the attention, and we certainly love those areas as you can tell from other parts of our book, New Orleans has other areas of equal beauty and significance.

Half-Shell Award: The Duvigneaud House

Located at 2857 Grand Route St. John (with an address like that, one's expectations are exceedingly high and the

Duvigneaud House does indeed surpass them), this is a charming and romantic bed and breakfast home in the classic New Orleans tradition. Built in 1834 and listed on the National Register of Historic Places, the home exudes a welcoming warmth. David Villarrubia restored it in the 1980s (he even went to France to research the Duvigneaud family) into a small B&B appointed with antique period pieces and yet comfortably spacious with modern conveniences.

In the heart of the Faubourg St. John, the Duvigneaud House is real butter at margarine prices. It is situated two blocks from the fairgrounds, four from the bayou with its majestic antebellum homes (a sketch of Pitot House is in this edition), four from City Park, three from True Brew Coffee and Whole Foods Market, four from a historic cemetery, and is a five-minute drive from the Quarter. Walking to these points is fine in the daytime only.

Kids are welcome, but pets and smoking are not permitted inside the home. Lie back on the swing on the porch or balcony and relax. Stay a while to save dollars (you get a discount, clothes washed, some meals in your suite) but a one-night stay is still a great deal and experience (821-5009).

The Degas House (1852) 2306 Esplanade (821-5009) In case you haven't figured it out yet the Faubourg St. John was home to the famous French impressionist Edgar Degas. And even if your *Half-Shell* authors were snubbed and received *no invitation to the Degas premiere benefit,* we decided that the establishment of the Degas Foundation was just too important to ignore. Besides, Degas himself probably wouldn't have attended his own benefit.

If we presume that all artists are eccentric, then Degas was the master. He painted over a dozen works while residing in New Orleans at what is now the Degas House. His mother was a New Orleans native and his father came from, you guessed it, France. Both wealthy, she from family cotton and he from banking, they financed Degas well to be as eccentric as he pleased. Any cursory study shows bouts of psychosis (sounds like your authors). But Degas liked New Orleans and once stated, "Louisiana must be respected by all her children of which I am almost one."

As appreciative as we are of art, we wonder why there has been no *major* Degas exhibit five blocks down the street at the New Orleans Museum of Art. Here is a treasure in our own backyard. Nothing against the Monet and other major exhibits but it seems odd to have to travel to Jackson, Mississippi to see the largest exhibit of Degas's sculpture. We know the fledgling Degas Foundation will work aggressively to educate the general public about the Degas legacy.

You can feel the artist's presence throughout the two-story Greek Revival Degas House. Masterful reproductions of his works are everywhere and even the painted walls reflect the colors he used. The first story, where Degas lived, houses the Degas Foundation. It consists of a museum and a gift shop where you can purchase posters, postcards, books and articles on Degas, and additional museum-quality remembrances. Personal tours and brochures are offered. You may want to relax on the back patio with a refreshment as well.

The second story of the Degas House is a cozy, traditional-type bed and breakfast with intimate rooms that accommodate mostly couples. It is appointed with a mixture of both period and reproduction antiques and rugs. The premier room sports a large balcony facing Esplanade Avenue, creating a real New Orleans atmosphere. It is very romantic at night, and interesting during the daytime with the passersby and denizens of the neighborhood.

The Fairchild House (1841) 1518 Prytania (1-800-256-8096 or 524-0154) A few years ago, owner Rita Olma Abrigliano, a native Brazilian and a city planner by profession, fell in love with Bob, followed him to New Orleans, and began a lifelong affair with our city (and with Bob). She had a vision for reviving this inner-city neighborhood. Just one block from the St. Charles streetcar; one block from Coliseum Square; a stone's throw from the art galleries, antique stores, secondhand shops, and funky flea markets on Magazine Street; and a short walk to the mansions of the Garden District, the Fairchild House, lovingly restored to its original Victorian charm, offers all the beauty and tranquility of the past, the warmth and hospitality of close-knit neighbors, and the excitement of our special New Orleans at your doorstep.

Bordered by Terpsichore and Euterpe—streets in the Lower Garden District—the house is fondly referred to by the manager and Rita's daughter, Beatrice, as "the place where the Muses meet." It is indeed a meeting place, with guests hailing from Brazil, Germany, Italy, Australia, and, of course, Texas. Upon arrival they are warmly welcomed by Beatrice herself or Alison, the night manager (who left in '93 but "just couldn't stay away"), personally escorted to the privacy of their rooms, and invited to partake of a lovely wine and cheese tray and enjoy the charm and romantic lighting of the garden patio or balcony.

Being literally a minute from the Rex and Bacchus parade routes and boasting a wrought-iron balcony that can accommodate 30 with available catering (or just a few for intimate weddings with candlelight and champagne), the house is extremely busy during Mardi Gras. Also from the balcony, you can feel the thunder and see the lightning of the annual Crescent City Classic footrace breaking the early-morning solitude, all while sipping champagne and Bloody Marys under the shade of the majestic gnarled live oaks that line "one of the prettiest streets in New Orleans."

You'll find no *Where Magazine* here. The staff are always current on what's happening in New Orleans, from music to cuisine, so that the guests, when not relaxing in the grandeur of the eight finely appointed rooms with private baths and gleaming hardwood floors, can fully enjoy the city's unique daytime and nighttime festivities. Continental breakfast is served each day in the "breakfast room," but a special added touch is afternoon teatime between 3:00 and 5:00 daily (except Sundays). The Fairchild House is not only a historical establishment but a reflection of the commitment, hard work, and dreams of a family who loves the city and its culture and wished to restore a jewel of the past for the enjoyment of future generations. English, French, Spanish, and Portuguese are spoken.

MOTELS

The place to find cheap motels is Airline Highway. This is the old highway to Baton Rouge and is an extension of Tulane Avenue. When the interstate highway was built and the traffic patterns shifted, the proliferation of motels fell on hard times. While we can't vouch for the quality, we can attest to the quantity. Rooms can be rented by the hour, for the day, or overnight. This variety of options is undoubtedly offered in an effort to attract truck drivers who must catch a few winks and be on their way. Ask to see the room before paying.

OTHER ACCOMMODATIONS

Lee Circle YMCA 936 St. Charles Ave. (568-9622)
Marquette House International Hostel 2253 Carondelet (523-3014)

Camping

There are several campgrounds located in the outlying areas, such as Chalmette and Slidell, and some in the New Orleans East area of Chef Menteur Highway. These are listed in the phone book. We would recommend the state park at Bayou Segnette (see **Recreation**).

It is illegal (and dangerous, as well) to sleep in the parks and at the lakefront areas. Don't try it! And don't, under any circumstances, sleep in other secluded areas you may find within the city itself. If you found it, chances are good others can, or will, also. These might not be people you would want to meet in a dark, out-of-the-way place.

Directory

Emergency

Traveler's Aid Society 525-8726
Visitor Information 566-5068
Legal Aid Bureau 523-2597
Emergency Medical Services 911
Suicide Prevention 1-800-333-4444
Rape Crisis Center.. 482-9922
Police   (New Orleans) 911
                (Jefferson Parish) 911
Jails   (New Orleans Police) 468-7270
                (Orleans Parish Sheriff) 827-8522
                (Jefferson Parish) 832-2484
To report a fire 911
Auto Pound (New Orleans)..244-4645
                (Jefferson Parish) 364-5350
Auto Towing Service ....(see **Twenty-four Hours**)

Hospitals

Charity Hospital	1532 Tulane Ave.	568-2311
Touro Infirmary	1401 Foucher St.	897-8250
Ochsner Hospital	1516 Jefferson Hwy.	842-3460
East Jefferson Hospital	4200 Houma Blvd.	454-4444
Homeless Central Clinic	914 Union	528-3750

Counseling and Guidance Services

Alcoholics Anonymous..525-1178
Battered Women's Program..486-0377
Battered Women's 24-Hour Line 837-5400
Substance Abuse Clinic 483-4883
AIDS Hotline 944-2437
AIDS Anonymous Center..488-1090

HIV Clinic 568-5304
STD Information 565-7700
Child Protection Hotline 483-4911/736-7033
Kids in Crisis Hotline 488-2955

Complaints

Taxicab Complaints 565-6272
Child Abuse 483-4911
Better Business Bureau 581-6222

Legal

Lawyer Referral Service 561-8828
Traffic Court   (New Orleans) 827-5091
                   (Jefferson Parish) 736-8900
Juvenile Court   (New Orleans)..................................565-7300
                   (Jefferson Parish) 367-3500
Arson Hot Line...822-1111
District Attorney (New Orleans) 822-2414
                   (Jefferson Parish) 368-1020

Social Services

Welfare Emergency Assistance 565-7155
Elderly Needing Transportation 523-5438
Salvation Army Men's Lodge 899-2332
Ozanam Inn 523-1184
Baptist Rescue Mission..523-5761
Covenant House (Runaways)..........................1-800-999-9999

Miscellaneous

Passports (New Orleans) 589-6161
          (Jefferson Parish) 364-2922
Youth Hostel 523-3014
YWCA 482-9922
YMCA 568-9622
Coroner..827-3575
League of Women Voters...581-9106

The Lay of the Land

The New Orleans metropolitan area is composed of several parishes, which the rest of the world calls "counties." Orleans Parish is the city of New Orleans. Jefferson Parish is to the west and is comprised of places called Metairie, Gretna, Kenner, and others to be noted later. These are the original "bedroom community" suburbs, but urban sprawl has rendered Jefferson and Orleans indistinguishable to the untrained eye. St. Bernard Parish is to the southeast and is also impossible to tell from New Orleans proper. Places with names like Chalmette, Arabi (one of our personal favorites, as geographical names go), and Violet (the home of the Violations) are in St. Bernard. The chic suburban communities are north of Lake Pontchartrain in St. Tammany Parish. Mandeville and Covington are the popular destinations for migration north of the lake.

The Mississippi River divides the metro area into the East Bank and the West Bank. A very small section of Orleans Parish, Old Algiers, is located on the West Bank of the river, and a large portion of Jefferson Parish is there. Jefferson communities located on the West Bank are Gretna, Harvey, Marrero, Westwego (West-we-go!!), and Avondale.

Many East Bankers consider the West Bank to be akin to Outer Mongolia and shudder to think of the uncivilized hordes who dwell therein. This attitude probably developed when the West Bank was primarily a group of fishing villages. Its perpetuation is no doubt largely due to the West Bank's accessibility problems.

Prior to 1988, two bridges traversed the river. The Huey P. Long Bridge is a product of the 1930s. An initial excursion on the narrow Huey P. can evoke more terror than any amusement park's best white-knuckle thrill ride. The Greater New Orleans Bridge is not nearly as old, but was not built to service the volume of traffic that eventually developed. A flat tire on a car going in either direction would snarl traffic for hours. A major accident created utter chaos.

In the fall of 1988, a parallel span to the GNO, which everyone seems to call "the New Bridge," opened. The dual spans were officially dubbed "The Crescent City Connection." Shortly thereafter, tolls, which had been removed several decades earlier, were reinstated ($1, payable on the West Bank approach). The toll booths slow down the morning commute only slightly and the crossing is infinitely easier and faster, even in the face of a breakdown or accident.

The gist of all this is that the West Bank should no longer be thought a hinterland. It is home to many upscale neighborhoods and a world-class Jack Nicklaus golf course at English Turn.

Old Algiers, on the West Bank, is the place where Jack Kerouac and Neal Cassady stopped over to visit with William Burroughs while in the midst of their odyssey that later became Kerouac's *On the Road*. The place has barely changed since "Bull Lee" lived here. In fact, it's hardly changed in the last hundred years.

Old Algiers is a small, architecturally attractive township. A walk through the unique environs of Algiers can provide an afternoon of relaxation and scenic distraction. To reach your destination, take the ferry that docks at Canal Street and the river, and 10 minutes later you're there. It's that simple.

MORE TRIVIA

New Orleans is an island surrounded by Lake Pontchartrain, drainage canals, and the Mississippi River.

The French Quarter and the Vieux Carré are one and the same.

New Orleans is called the Crescent City due to the fact that it's built on a bend in the Mississippi River.

Iberville and Bienville founded and developed the city around 1718.

We are one of the busiest ports in the United States.

Levees and canals are the only barriers that prevent New Orleans from being underwater.

Getting Around

Where We At?

One afternoon at the Riverbend, where St. Charles and Carrollton meet, a visitor who was trying to get his bearings asked us which direction was north. While most can generally ascertain the direction of Florida and California and then by process of elimination figure out north, some of the most educated New Orleanians would stumble at the question. Because we are located at a bend in the Mississippi River, conventional directions don't work. Driving from the East Bank to the West Bank with the early-morning sun in one's face can confuse even a boy scout with a compass.

For directions, we use downtown, uptown, the river, and the lake. Canal Street is the basic dividing line between downtown and uptown. Anything on the French Quarter side of Canal is downtown. The other side is uptown. The river and lake are so dominating that their directions are obvious. You might be confused when someone tells you that he lives on the downtown, lake side of a certain intersection, but a local would nod and say, "Yeah, my gawdmama stays ova' by you."

Getting around the city is a relatively easy process, whether you have your own means of transportation or choose to use public transit.

NEUTRAL GROUNDS

These are actually wide strips of land running down the middle of a street, separating the street into two sides. During the colonial period of New Orleans, some of these neutral grounds were used to peacefully separate the French from the Spanish, the Spanish from the English, etc., etc. Specific historic examples are Canal Street, Esplanade Avenue, and Elysian Fields.

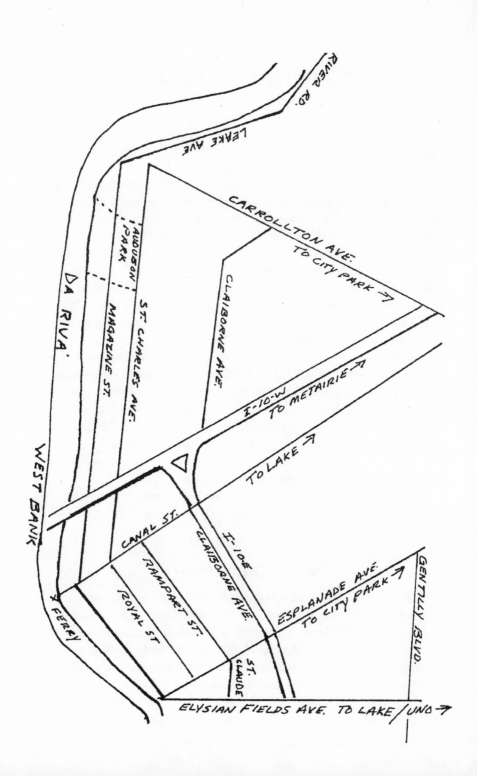

The Regional Transit Authority

The RTA operates the local bus and streetcar system. It runs to every part of the city, and many lines run 24 hours. The fare is $1 and rising. There are also passes available on a daily, weekly, or monthly basis. These allow unlimited service for the specified period of time, thus enabling the visitor to take side trips and re-board streetcars and buses. For information call RTA (569-2700).

The St. Charles streetcar runs from Canal Street up St. Charles to Carrollton Avenue, and on to Claiborne Avenue. At the end of the line the route is reversed. It's an excellent way to see uptown New Orleans!

If you like the St. Charles streetcar—and you will—check out its Riverfront cousin. With the development of the New Orleans riverfront came the necessity of transporting the crowds between the attractions. The solution was to appropriate one of the old rail lines that passes through the area and put a streetcar on it. Our newest streetcar line runs from Esplanade at the back of the French Quarter to Erato Street in

the Warehouse District. The route services the French Quarter, Jax Brewery, the Aquarium of the Americas and Woldenberg Park, the Riverwalk, and the Convention Center.

In addition to the bus and streetcar services, other traditional methods of transportation are available. Taxis are abundant and most are good; United Cab is recommended. The usual car-rental agencies are also readily accessible.

Streets

Negotiating the streets of the city isn't difficult. One can get to nearly any location by utilizing a few main arteries. Since everyone can and does go to the French Quarter, we will use it as a point of reference.

To go **Uptown**, which is technically across Canal Street from the French Quarter, the main arteries are Magazine Street and St. Charles Avenue. Magazine Street runs from Canal and Decatur to the river at Audubon Park. "The Street of Dreams," as it is known, is home to every type of small shop imaginable, especially art galleries and antique stores. One of the most colorful streets in the city, Magazine intersects many New Orleans neighborhoods. These include a large Latin community, the Garden District, the Lower Garden District, the Irish Channel, and the University section.

St. Charles Avenue is probably New Orleans' most celebrated and scenic avenue. Running from Royal and Canal, St. Charles parallels Magazine Street to the Mississippi River and makes a right turn into Carrollton Avenue, which then continues to City Park. St. Charles is the home of elegant mansions, beautiful trees, Audubon Park, and the Tulane and Loyola university campuses.

To go in another direction from the French Quarter, to the **Lake Pontchartrain area**, a major route is Canal Street. Canal begins at the river and runs the entire river-to-lake length of the

BEST OVERPASS: Lakeshore Drive at Bayou St. John

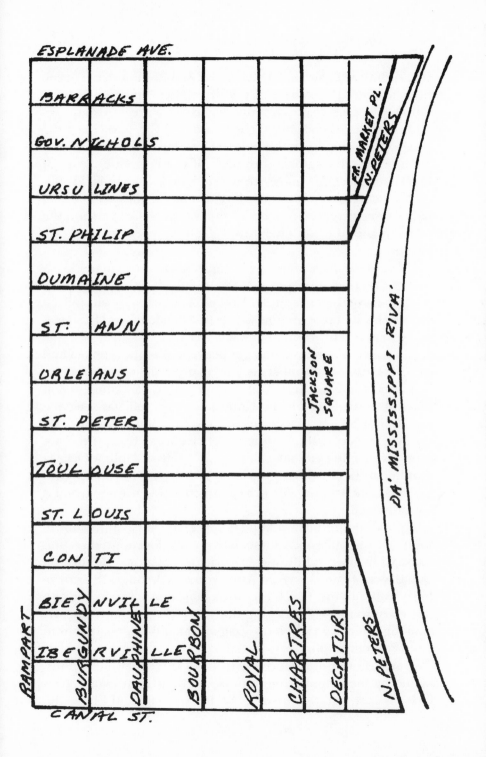

city, ending at Lakeshore Drive (via Canal Boulevard). In addition to being the center of the downtown business district, Canal Street has many charming residential areas. Two neighborhoods that Canal goes through are Mid-City and Lakeview.

Also running from the river to the lake is Elysian Fields Avenue, which begins at the back of the French Quarter at Esplanade Avenue and North Peters Street. Elysian Fields traverses the neighborhoods of Marigny and Gentilly and ends at Lakeshore Drive, where the University of New Orleans and the ruins of the old Pontchartrain Beach Amusement Park are located.

Using these four major thoroughfares and the major cross streets that they intersect, a traveler can get to basically every part of the city. Of course, this is an extremely simplified approach, but these are the streets that can keep you from getting lost and return you to familiar territory.

There are very few ways to get between the uptown area and the City Park/Lakefront areas. The main route of Carrollton to St. Charles and vice versa can get uncomfortably congested at major intersections. The best alternatives are Jeff Davis Avenue and Canal Street. If you are above Louisiana Avenue, go uptown to Nashville Avenue and drive away from the river. When Nashville ends, take a right and a left and follow Octavia as it becomes Jeff Davis Avenue. It runs along Bayou St. John to Esplanade Avenue. The drive is much less aggravating, and is scenic as well.

A good nighttime and holiday route, if you're on the downtown side of Louisiana Avenue, is to go in a downtown direction through the Central Business District to Canal Street. Turn on Canal away from the river. After you get through the downtown traffic lights, which are not a major annoyance because there are so many interesting things to see, you have a nearly straight (there's a right-left zigzag at Canal Boulevard) shot to Lake Pontchartrain.

Traveling to the **Eastern** environs of this great metropolis, including the neighborhoods of Bywater, the Ninth Ward, New Orleans East, and the thriving hamlets of Arabi and Chalmette in St. Bernard Parish, is a simple matter also. You need only utilize a few major arteries to arrive at your destination. From the French Quarter, drive out either Esplanade Avenue or Elysian Fields Avenue and you will cross all the main roads heading east. The first, St. Claude Avenue, will take you through Bywater, the Ninth Ward, Arabi, and finally into Chalmette. This is a straight shot; there's no getting lost. Another direct route to Chalmette is Claiborne Avenue, a few blocks farther up from St. Claude. (Incidentally, Chalmette is the site of the infamous Battle of New Orleans, which took place after the Treaty of Ghent, ending the War of 1812, had already been signed!)

New Orleans East is the newest suburban area of New Orleans. This is best reached by Interstate 10. I-10 East (or I-610) can be found intersecting Elysian Fields Avenue. The exits Morrison Road, Crowder Boulevard, Read Boulevard, and Bullard Road are the heart of New Orleans East, which is, in reality, just another suburb.

Farther out Elysian Fields, past I-10, is Gentilly Boulevard. Take a right to go through the neighborhood of Gentilly (the setting for Walker Percy's 1962 National Book Award-winning novel, *The Moviegoer*), and shortly the street name changes to Chef Menteur Highway. The Chef, as it is known locally, is the home of several of the more inexpensive motels in the city. It will also take you to the older areas of New Orleans East.

Traffic Alert

As in most large cities, driving in New Orleans during the peak traffic hours (7 to 9 A.M. and 4 to 6 P.M.) is no fun. The A.M. traffic coming into town from Metairie, the West Bank, and New Orleans East moves at a crawl at best. The afternoon traffic outbound in the same directions is nothing short of a nightmare. The drive to avoid at all costs is I-10 East toward Slidell. The high-rise bridge over the Industrial Canal is the nemesis of large trucks. Whether coming or going, they seem to give out with startling regularity on the upgrade. Traffic backs up for miles. A couple of hours sitting here on a hot afternoon is the closest thing to hell we can imagine.

Hitchhiking

Hitchhiking used to be a good way to get around, meet people, and have fun back in the late sixties and early seventies. Now that we've lived through the eighties and entered the nineties, hitchhiking is just plain dangerous. Even though all things hip in the sixties seem to be making a comeback (witness the proliferation of ponytails on guys and tie dye), hitchhiking is best left as a memory of another time, not only in New Orleans, but probably everywhere.

If you refuse to follow the sage advice just rendered, at least stand on the curb and not in the street. While there may be some city ordinances that prohibit the practice of "thumbing a ride," they are rarely (and perhaps selectively) enforced. Use your own judgment as to whether you choose to do this, and if you have any doubts, don't.

Getting In and Out of Town

New Orleans is served by all the usual methods of national transit. The Trailways and Greyhound **bus lines** and **Amtrak** operate out of the same facility: the Union Passenger Terminal. This is located where Howard Avenue, Loyola Avenue, and Earhart Boulevard all come together. While waiting for your train or bus, have a look at the four murals that adorn the walls of the terminal. These works, completed in 1954, depict 400 years of Louisiana's history, including events current at the time of the painting.

New Orleans International Airport is approximately 12 miles from downtown. The easiest and most inexpensive methods of access are the limousine and minibus services. These serve most of the larger hotels. Call 469-4555 for information.

Food

This section of our book is *not* about Antoine's, Commander's Palace, or Galatoire's—wondrous gourmet food at astronomical prices. (Hint: If you're inclined to try these anyway, Commander's is the best, particularly the garden room, and go at lunch for real savings.) It is about exceptional restaurants that fall in the low- to moderate-price range and offer just as high quality food and fast service as the higher-priced spreads. Many of these neighborhood restaurants are real gems frequented by the most savvy locals. So now you can save yourself a lot of money. Your purchase of our book has paid for itself many times over. What a great stocking stuffer *New Orleans on the Half-Shell* would be. You're welcome!

The Traditional Neighborhood Restaurant

What is the essence of the New Orleans neighborhood restaurant? Various esoteric requirements should be met to satisfy the designation. The characteristic restaurant must:

1. Serve generous portions of delicious food and drink.

2. Have a distinct charm of its own (even a tacky one).

3. Exude an inviting ambience that attracts a diverse socioeconomic array of customers (a magnet for the mayor and day laborer alike, with equal dining comfort for both).

4. Contain nothing fancy or pretentious (consider tablecloths the exception and darkened crust on the lips of hot-sauce bottles the rule).

5. Accept both casual and formal attire as de rigueur (T-shirt and jeans or tails and top hat).

6. Have low to moderate prices whereby the entire family might dine without leasing a child to cover the check.

7. Employ someone who has, over the years, come to be

41

known as a local institution of sorts (e.g., a waiter, bartender, owner, or cook).

8. Present an exterior of somewhat dubious appearance that may cause the unknowing patron to wonder about the authors' sanity or sobriety (not to worry—some of our best eating establishments are real dumps).

MID-CITY

Half-Shell Award: Katie's

Katie's bills itself as the neighborhood restaurant for the entire city. While this is quite an assertion to make, we have come to agree and therefore bestow on Katie's one of our rare Half-Shell Awards. Situated at the corner of Telemachus (just what the hell is a Telemachus, anyway?) and Iberville Street, Katie's rests in the heart of Mid-City (which isn't in the middle of the city). Katie's is actually only a couple of blocks from world-famous Mandina's and from the equally great New Orleans favorite, Liuzza's (only during the daylight hours should you venture on foot to any of these).

Katie's is different. It is actually a very nicely appointed restaurant, which you might think is contradictory to being characterized as a "neighborhood restaurant." So? We can do that. Literary license and all that. Remember this is a neighborhood restaurant for the whole city. Think how weird that sounds. And its owner, Scott Craig, is himself a local institution of sorts and serves up a sumptuous menu of indigenous delights. So welcome to *the* traditional, nontraditional N'Awlins neighborhood restaurant, whose listing on the back of the menu you will find extraordinary.

Katie's boasts a bevy of specialties. Some are on the menu, but we never order from the menu, because the chalkboard specials posted daily are sure things. (For instance, crawfish étouffée is not on the menu, Mr. Food Critic, but we defy you to find one better.)

Okay, okay, we lied. We have ordered off the menu too. You can't go wrong with the Italian specials, the seafood, or the po' boys. And are you ready for this? Katie's special Sicilian hamburger with both mozzarella cheese and marinara sauce is unsurpassed.

The all-homemade desserts are simply scrumptious. We prefer the bread pudding, but where else can you get peach cobbler and cannoli on the same menu? And we don't like to tell too many people about this but here goes: Katie's happy-hour double shots of good well drinks go for less than $3. Thanks, Scott, and what a great staff you have! Katie's is located at 3701 Iberville St. (488-6582).

Highlight: Mandina's, The Quintessential Neighborhood Restaurant

If we were requested to recommend a superb restaurant at the right price for a newcomer, tourist, or native, Mandina's would be our automatic answer. Hey, where else can you eat a wonderfully messy po' boy, sip turtle soup au sherry, and order imported wine at 1970s prices, all in a neighborhood restaurant? We kid you not.

The service at Mandina's is fast, attentive, and nearly as great as the food. With any kind of luck at all you might be asked to wait for your table at the stand-up bar, where you will probably rub shoulders with a judge, Saint (the football variety), TV anchor, or local neighborhood resident. And if you're very lucky, it will be the neighborhood resident.

Seafood appetizers (especially the generous Shrimp Remoulade) and soups (oyster/artichoke and turtle) are fresh and stimulating. Tasty oysters and shrimp provide substantial fillings for the seafood po' boys and are fried in separate vats to capture the unique flavor of each. But, oh, the marinated crab claws! They are a garlic lover's delight. Served hot with a dripping well-seasoned butter sauce, they are a meal in themselves, just begging for you to dip in with your French bread, which is, of course, always fresh at Mandina's.

Daily luncheon and dinner specials are highly recommended. Try the Fish Marguerite when available. Mandina's exhibits a special touch with soft-shell crabs as well. Bread pudding for dessert is one in a series of New Orleans prototypes.

Mandina's, through character, price, and quality, meets all of the requirements of the quintessential New Orleans neighborhood restaurant. Valet parking seems strange for this neighborhood jewel but just adds to its extraordinary character. Mandina's is located at 3800 Canal St., between the cemeteries and downtown (482-9179).

Highlight: Liuzza's

Liuzza's, a boiled crab's throw from Katie's and also on the corner of Telemachus, rounds out the loop of the taste-sational triumvirate of Mid-City restaurants, all within seconds of each other. In fact, during the daytime, you might want to try the soup and salad at Mandina's, walk two blocks and sample an array of appetizers at Katie's, and then ramble a few yards to Liuzza's, where you can split an entrée topped off by dessert. Since you won't be able to move after a scrumptious meal at Liuzza's, it is definitely the place to hang out for the afternoon, take in some televised sports at the bar, and enjoy a giant frozen schooner and the local camaraderie, all before one of the city's better beer happy hours. And where else can you get frozen Bushwhackers this side of Pensacola as well as giant schooners of root beer for the kids?

Drifting from the talented kitchen of Liuzza's is the scent of ageless recipes, which can be savored throughout the neighborhood. Italian, seafood, and special dishes remain the easy way to go. Try the Frenchuletta, a muffuletta on French bread and enough for two to split; it's a creative alternative to the traditional muffuletta and combines the best of our city's French and Italian culinary delights. Liuzza's has added extra well lit off-street parking in the rear for convenience and a security guard for nighttime parking. Liuzza's is located at 3636 Bienville (482-9120).

College Inn 3016 South Carrollton (866-3683) You don't need a degree to read this extensive menu. From luncheon specials and po' boys to complete dinners, College Inn continues to provide great food for local families and couples. You can go alone, too, but it helps to have assistance with the large order of onion rings. Highly recommended by us since our 1981 street edition.

Dooky Chase's 2301 Orleans (821-0600) Some of the best Creole food in the city. Although popular with local politicos, don't let that deter you from the lunch specials or take-out food. Located at the bottom of the expressway (I-10) and across from the projects.

Lola's 3312 Esplanade (488-6946) This is the newcomer to the group of escape-type eateries in the Faubourg St. John area. The food is hearty, unpretentious, and well seasoned. Lola's doesn't exactly categorize itself as a Spanish restaurant, but the paellas for two are excellent. Come early or late—it seems the restaurant is always overflowing with diners spilling out onto the sidewalk, enjoying wine (brought from home) and conversation as they wait for tables.

Louisiana Pizza Kitchen 2808 Esplanade (488-2800) Although part of a chain, this Esplanade Avenue restaurant cannot be omitted here due to the architecture of the building and the quality of the pizza. They serve much more than wonderful pizzas (not Pizza Hut or Domino's type—try the garlic, feta cheese, and spinach on for size), including interesting Italian dishes and great salads.

Palmer's, 135 N. Carrollton Ave. (482-3658) Chef Cecil Palmer brought his recipes from his native Jamaica. The dishes include curried goat, jerked fish, and bahamian chowder. This is a best bet.

BUCKTOWN/WEST END/LAKEVIEW

Half-Shell Award: Sid-Mar's

Mon Dieu, if this isn't the best, most consistent seafood restaurant in metropolitan New Orleans, then them crawdad haids ain't for suckin'. Sid-Mar's gets a Half-Shell Award for ambience, service, and unparalleled fried seafood. Miriam Gemelli Burgess, the owner, and Ruth Varisco, her cousin (and incidentally, an instructor in the Nunez College Culinary Department), call it "healthy cooking." How so? you protest. Miriam uses only corn oil and nothing is precooked. And you can tell!

The melt-in-your-mouth fried platter, which is served in the traditional fashion on top of toast points (oysters, crab claws, shrimp, onion rings), is outstanding, and the whole artichoke, steamed, very lightly breaded, and spectacularly seasoned, is by far the best artichoke dish in the city. Seafood gumbo (one of the best-selling items, along with the seafood po' boy and the chicken Bordelaise) is, like all the soups, made from scratch, but our favorites are the silky seafood bisque and the unrivaled crab and corn. Sid-Mar's (which stands for Sidney's and Miriam's) is one of the few restaurants where you can still get a "wop salad" (which is delicious), and considering the heritage of this family-owned establishment, we defy you to make a comment.

A feature of this home-style restaurant that keeps the regulars coming is the lunch special. Under $5 and served every Tuesday to Friday, this has become a Sid-Mar's institution. Every day it's a different treat—crawfish étouffée, baked macaroni, shrimp Creole—but try to be there Thursday. It's Italian day, when Miriam serves up such delights as lasagna and stuffed manicotti.

It's not just the food that lures you here. It's the personalities past and present, the history, the screened porch at water's edge, the funky tilting men's room (which no one wants them to change), the stories, the resident ducks and birds on the levee, and it's Old Bucktown, a historic landmark, one tiny remaining block beside the water speckled with fishing boats, reminiscent of another era. Miriam caters to the fishermen and they have always reciprocated with the freshest of catches for the restaurant. Sid-Mar's is located at 1824 Orpheum (831-9541).

SEAFOOD TO GO

If you enjoyed the shrimp, crabs, and crawfish, then take some home with you when you depart. Near Bucktown there are a number of seafood houses that pack seafood in portable dry-ice containers. Try Deanie's Seafood, 1713 Lake Ave. (835-4638), Captain Sid's, 1700 Lake (831-2840), or Schaefer and Rusich, 1726 Lake (833-3973). Check the Yellow Pages under "Seafood—Retail" for more locations.

Highlight: Mona Lisa

The Lakeview Mona Lisa is not quite the "hole in the wall" that the original Quarter location is, but the food is every bit as delicious, prepared under the meticulous and watchful eye of Fatma Ayden, co-owner and manager. Fatma, arriving from Turkey in 1986, joined her brother who had already settled here. Both she and her brother (who now also owns Cafe Istanbul, in the Faubourg Marigny) had been working in restaurants to make ends meet as new immigrants to New Orleans. When a property became available, Fatma said, "Why don't we open a restaurant?" The rest is history.

The cuisine is Italian with an interesting Middle Eastern flair. Garlic bread looks like a pizza without the tomato sauce and is a delicious house favorite (don't order too much; you won't be able to finish your dinner). We like the romaine salad with fresh grated mozzarella, tomatoes, tangy Greek olives, mushrooms, and green peppers. Topped by a wonderful house dressing with a feta-cheese base, this and the garlic bread is a meal for two. The salad gets better as you go and the dressing seeps into the vegetables.

The pasta dishes are breathtaking, and boast subtle flavors that make them interestingly different from those of other Italian restaurants. The eggplant parmesan, for example, is baked, light, and smothered in a delightful almost-sweet red sauce. The seafood pasta, on the other hand, with fresh fish (redfish), shrimp, clams, and a magnificent lemon-butter sauce, is spicy with just enough garlic to tantalize. A favorite with the crowd that frequents Mona Lisa is the Mardi Gras Pasta, a superb combination of sausage, linguine, shrimp, and a hearty, different-flavored red sauce. Quite different from the average Italian fare is the lasagna, which is not exactly layers of pasta but is stuffed with generous amounts of meat or spinach.

Diners tend to eat early at this establishment and it's already full by 7:00. The wine selection by the glass is decent and extremely reasonable. We suggest the Chianti at $2.75 a glass. Mona Lisa is located at 874 Harrison Ave. (488-0133).

R&O 210 Old Hammond Hwy. (831-1248) We've been touting the merits of this Bucktown restaurant for years—way before they moved from around the corner to their present location on the levee. Po' boys, especially the oyster, shrimp, roast beef, meatball, and sausage, are among the very best in the city. The R&O special, ham and roast beef with melted provolone cheese, is a favorite. The pizza, their original claim to fame, is still superb. Many think R&O's seafood gumbo is the best in the city. They have an excellent variation of bread pudding, also. (Authors' note: One mainstream New Orleans food critic writes that the "atmosphere is nothing to write home about." Well, if you want atmosphere, eat at Arnaud's [sounds like R&O's]. If you want fabulous New Orleans food where you can take out a family of five without taking out a second mortgage, eat at R&O's.)

West End Cafe 8536 Pontchartrain Blvd. (288-0711) This family-friendly neighborhood spot is located just a block from where much of our original book was written. Once again, a good place for sandwiches, specials, and boiled seafood.

Russell's Marina Grill 8555 Pontchartrain Blvd. (282-9980) Russell's Marina Grill has quickly developed an outstanding reputation for breakfast as well as lunch and dinner. Look for the daily specials, the omelets, and the classic hamburger that is a renaissance piece among burgers. Don't exit without trying the onion mum. Here's a valuable hint: we've never had anything short of good here.

Landry's 789 Harrison Ave. (488-6496) In the same neighborhood where the old Beacon and Lakeview theaters stood, Landry's serves up delicious daily lunches in a vintage setting. Oysters on the half-shell are always available. On the corner across from St. Dominic's Catlick Church. Drive by and read their chalkboard on the street for today's lunch!

Lakeview Harbor 911 Harrison Ave. (486-4887) This is a strange but successful combination of a restaurant offering great dishes to local families and a fabulous neighborhood bar boasting an equally fabulous jukebox. You can eat the same dishes at the bar and, to enjoy local color, that's what we prefer to do. One of the best baked potatoes to be had can be found here—they're loaded and usually accompany the huge sandwiches. (Chicken is our favorite but the hamburger rivals that of specialty establishments. Move over, Port of Call.)

Authors' Tip: The Progressive 3-Hour Lunch (a la neighborhood) —Begin with raw oysters at **Landry's**. Hop in your car and drive to **Sid-Mar's** for a portion of crawfish. Walk over to **R&O's** for a soft-shell crab po' boy. Go ahead, order the bread pudding here because it's good and you probably can't move anyway. Drive to **West End Cafe** for an after-lunch Dixie. Cross the street to **Russell's Marina Grill** for coffee with chicory. Hedonism at its best! If you split the bills with a partner or go with half-orders, then the cost of this splurge is a lot less than you might think. Now you've sampled five restaurants in a most adventuresome fashion.

UPTOWN

Parasol's 2533 Constance (899-2054) Deep in the heart of the Irish Channel, near the Garden District, Parasol's is the definitive New Orleans neighborhood restaurant as well as the historical king of the po' boys. We remember one Monday a student from New Jersey attempted to order a "red beans and rice with sausage po' boy." When the cook's laughter subsided, the student was counseled to order the roast beef po' boy, the "best in the city." When he demanded the plate of beans and rice the cook responded, "We gon' give ya dat too, dawlin'—fer nuttin'." Go to Parasol's on St. Patrick's Day and partake of green beer before viewing the parade!

Blue Bird Cafe 3625 Prytania (895-7166) The Uptown "Bird" has established itself as the place for weekday breakfasts and *huevos rancheros* on weekends. The daily specials are extraordinary and inexpensive. Second location on Panola too.

Franky & Johnny's 321 Arabella (899-9146) Specials abound at this neighborhood restaurant and bar. The emphasis is on seafood, both fried and boiled. You can't go wrong at Franky & Johnny's.

Norby's 6078 Laurel (895-9441) A great neighborhood restaurant tucked away Uptown, offering typical working-man's lunches, New Orleans style. Po' boys are a plus here as well. This is the location of the famous wheelbarrow races held once a year by the charged but friendly Tulane-LSU football fanatics.

Streetcar Sandwiches 1434 S. Carrollton Ave. (866-1146) Eat inside or at the sidewalk tables, take 'em home, or even have them delivered, but whatever you do, get a sandwich from this Uptown eatery. The grill is stoked with the popular mesquite wood, giving the grilled sandwiches a distinctive flavor not normally found in a po' boy.

METAIRIE

Come Back Inn 8016 W. Metairie (467-9316) This is a traditional New Orleans neighborhood restaurant specializing in daily lunches and po' boys. The roast beef and the hot sausage are the best. Come Back Inn is rapidly becoming an institution in Metairie. Located between David Drive and Williams Boulevard.

Alonso's 587 Central (733-2796) It's hard to find (situated between the tracks and Jefferson Highway), but well worth the effort. Try the specials and the delightful fried seafood po' boys.

Giorlando's 741 Bonnabel (835-8593) Po' boys, daily lunches, and even muffulettas. Right off Veterans Highway.

Parran's 3939 Veterans Hwy. (885-3416) Plate lunches and po' boys. Still doing well after all these years.

The Louisiana Seafood Exchange 428 Jefferson Hwy. (834-9395) A fish market and sandwich shop just across da parish line. The seafood sandwiches are stuffed so full that the filling falls out of the bread. In fact, there is usually twice as much fallout as stuffing. The seafood muffuletta has been voted best sandwich in the city by the readers of the weekly newspaper, *Gambit*. For about $10, this monster is a meal for 4 with shrimp, oysters, or whatever else they can cram into the 12-inch round loaf of bread.

THE QUARTER

Mena's Palace 622 Iberville (525-0217) This is the lunch place for great food, large portions, and cheap prices. The specials range from sandwiches to meals. Breakfast, lunch, *and* dinner at Mena's will cost you less than $15.

Cafe Maspero 601 Decatur at Toulouse (523-6250) The best "stuffed" sandwich and the best deal in the Quarter are undeniably served up at Maspero's. The sandwiches are served on French buns and stuffed to overflowing with roast beef, ham, pastrami, or just about any other filling you can imagine. The only drawback to this place is the crowd. Expect to stand in line at peak hours and all afternoon on weekends. Be patient—you'll be glad you waited. Don't be fooled by imitators.

Napoleon House 500 Chartres St. (524-9752) The food is excellent and the atmosphere is unsurpassed in the Western hemisphere. See **Civilized Pleasure**s.

Vera Cruz 1141 Decatur St. (561-8081) Respectable Mexican food and deadly margaritas. Uptown, too!

Castillo's 620 Conti (525-7467) Real Mexican cuisine without the Tex-Mex influence. Margaritas made with fresh-squeezed lime juice.

OTHER RECOMMENDED NEIGHBORHOOD
RESTAURANTS

Highlight: The Bon Ton, the Big Splurge

If you want to celebrate a special occasion or just experience one of our classic Creole restaurants, the Bon Ton is the place to do it. This is the type of place where New Orleanians have had dinner every Friday night for 20 years. The atmosphere is classic New Orleans, with the food servers in starched whites. The food ranks with the best Creole dishes in the city. The value is beyond compare, with full meals at about $20. The Redfish Bon Ton and the étouffées are highly recommended. The Bon Ton is located at 401 Magazine (524-3386).

Mother's 401 Poydras (523-9656) Do not miss Mother's. Simply one of the best. Try the Ferdi Special or the hot lunch. The gumbo is super.

Uglesich's 1238 Baronne (523-8571) A popular neighborhood restaurant offering an array of seafood and especially oyster dishes. Eat 'em raw, fried, or in one of the house specials. If oysters aren't to your liking, try the spicy Shrimp Uggie.

The Praline Connection 542 Frenchmen (943-3934) Everyone who grew up south of I-10 (and we could probably extend this northward to I-20) needs to have turnip greens and corn bread on occasion. If you haven't had your soul food fix in a while, we suggest you head down to the Praline Connection in the Faubourg Marigny. The fried chicken might be the best you've ever eaten.

Eddie's 2119 Law (945-2207) A visit to Eddie's used to be one of the requirements for a New Orleans culture course offered by a local university. Their lunch and dinner specials are hard to beat. The beans and rice, stuffed pork chops, fried chicken, and seafood are excellent *Food & Wine* magazine rates the gumbo at Eddie's as the best in New Orleans. We go a step farther and rate it as one of the top three in the hemisphere (of course the other two gumbos are from New Orleans, too).

Mandich 3200 St. Claude (947-9553) Mandich specializes in New Orleans cuisine, with exceptional seafood dishes and another outstanding version of bread pudding. It's somewhat costlier than most neighborhood spots, however.

Rocky and Carlo's 613 W. St. Bernard Hwy. (279-8323) Way out in Chalmette, where the accent is on cheap, tasty, and huge helpings. Order the baked macaroni and feed the family for a week.

If It's Monday, It's Red Beans and Rice Day

On Mondays in New Orleans we're all recovering from the weekend. There is a surefire method to revitalize the spirit at noon. Each Monday, lunchtime means red beans and rice cooked the Creole way.

From fine dining establishments to neighborhood restaurants, "seasoned" cooks stir the simmering and creamy Camellia red beans. The painstaking process takes several attentive hours. When properly prepared, the beans form their own tasty sauce and are always ladled over a hot bed of rice. The delicious dish is an ancient institution and is usually cooked and served with sausage, ham hocks, pork chops, or pickled pork seasoning. French bread and hot sauce are the only accompaniments to this rib-sticking standard. Yes, siesta time may be necessary, and if you have to return to the job, your productivity will be minimal. This ain't no dainty and elegant dish. We're talking hearty.

Every native was weaned on these magical beans. School cafeterias have served this traditional dish every Monday since Horace Mann. Incidentally, if your plate of red beans and rice costs more than 5 bucks, then the price should include a Barq's or a Dixie at least. Otherwise, you're in the wrong place!

Today's Menu

Red beans
and Rice

Fried chicken

greens and
Corn bread

Great red beans and rice may be found throughout the city. Unfortunately, you might run into poor examples of the dish, too (beware of any Creole restaurant run by a couple from Hamburg, Iowa, for example). A rule of thumb is that the beans should not be chewy. They need to be well seasoned and flavorful, but not chock-full of such an inferno of spices that they are indistinguishable from the cayenne. A bay leaf on your platter is a positive sign. Any of our neighborhood restaurants (see listing under *The Traditional Neighborhood Restaurant*) are recommended for red beans and rice, but we *highly* recommend the following:

NEIGHBORHOOD

Eddie's 2119 Law (945-2207)

Mother's 401 Poydras (523-9656)

Ye Olde College Inn 3016 S. Carrollton (866-3683)

Spitale's 2408 N. Arnoult (837-9912)

OTHER HIGHLY RECOMMENDED RESTAURANTS

Dooky Chase's 2301 Orleans (821-2294)

*****Gumbo Shop** 630 St. Peter (525-1486)

*****Popeyes** This is a fast-food chain with some of the best red beans and rice in the world for around $1 for a small serving. Check the Yellow Pages for the nearest of their 10 million locations.

*****Copeland's** Several locations (Yellow Pages again), but the one at 4338 St. Charles is our favorite (897-2325).

*It doesn't have to be Monday at these restaurants because they serve red beans and rice anytime!

A Hero *Ain't* a Muffuletta!

DATELINE: NEW YORK—The Big Apple's premier newspaper, that bastion of progressive journalism and investigative savoir faire, dudn' no nuttin' 'bout eatin' in da Big Easy. We wish that *The New York Times*, which courageously revealed the truth about Vietnam in Ellsberg's *Pentagon Papers* exposé, would return to accuracy in reporting, especially about something as serious as our incomparable muffuletta sandwich (pronounced "muff-a-lettah" or "moof-a-lottah," depending on the neighborhood). Here is our case in point: the *Times* "covered" the New Orleans Jazz and Heritage Festival recently. A gourmet reporter was even dispatched from the cherry cocktail island called Manhattan to uncover the indigenous foods offered at the Fest. The description of our Creole and Cajun cuisine provided the reader with the best of plain brown wrapper generic coverage, a style that is doubtless accepted, if not applauded, by The City's populace. However, the worst offense was saved for the summary: the N'awlins muffuletta, unique among the species dubbed "sandwich," the pride of the working class and elite alike, was classified by the world's most famous rag as a *hero sandwich!*

"All the news that's fit to print." Indeed. A sacrilege. Words that will live in infamy. Have you ever had a hero sandwich? Ho hum. Yawn. The sandwich of the Big Bland.

Being gracious Southern gentlemen, we shall pardon this faux pas of colossal magnitude. We invite our visiting brothers and sisters of York de Nouveau to join the natives in sinking their teeth into a mighty muffuletta (usually large enough for two to share).

When you initially taste the fresh-baked brown crusty layer of this circular sesame-seeded Italian roll with the thick white bread interior, you know a hero is no muffuletta. Your sandwich *extraordinaire* is 26 inches or more in circumference and usually halved or quartered to reveal nearly an inch of assorted sliced meats, generously covered with melted provolone or mozzarella cheese. And now the coup de grace: a marinated Italian olive salad spread scrumptiously throughout.

The muffuletta is a sandwich to make the Earl himself smile with satisfied delight. The muffuletta is a hero of a sandwich, but definitely not a hero. It's in a class of its own.

THE CITY'S BEST

Central Grocery 923 Decatur (523-1620) The muffuletta originated here nearly a century ago, and C.G. is still #1.

Progress Grocery 915 Decatur, close to Central Grocery (news traveled fast) (525-6627)

Napoleon House 500 Chartres (524-9752) First in atmosphere and great muffulettas.

Is a Po' Boy a Poor Boy?

Yeah, ya right, bra! And we are definitely not talking socio-economics here. A po' boy is a New Orleans sandwich institution. Normally a po' boy is a foot or more of French bread with any of a number of fillings: roast beef (sandwich must be full of homemade gravy and nearly impossible to pick up because of all the debris falling out), fried oyster (try an oyster loaf), fried shrimp, sausage (hot, smoked, or Italian), barbecued beef, ham, veal cutlet, soft-shell crab, and even potato! When you place your order, "dressed" refers to lettuce, tomato, and "mynez," which is Yat vernacular (see later chapter) for mayonnaise. At last count you could order a po' boy at hundreds of establishments in the Greater New Orleans area. The po' boy is a gastronomical sensation and an economical delight.

THE BEST OF THE PO' BOYS (not including those listed
   under *The Traditional Neighborhood Restaurant*)
   Short Stop 119 Transcontinental (Metairie) (885-4572)
   Johnny's 511 St. Louis (French Quarter) (524-8129)
   Domilise's 5340 Annunciation (899-9126)
   Weaver's 800 Navarre Ave. (488-9267)

Motha Roux—Gumbo, or What?!

The *American Heritage Dictionary* describes "gumbo" as a "Louisiana soup or stew thickened with okra." Then they don't even define "roux." Well, mudda roux! A roux is a base for most Cajun and Creole cooking. The ingredients for a roux are usually quite easy to remember: butter or shortening and flour. That's it! However, the complexities of correctly making the roux demand a seasoned cook. A roux must be heated to an exact temperature, and it may be red, brown, or nearly black, depending on the dish. Not so easy, huh?

Now, you have to have the right roux even to attempt gumbo, so we find it much easier to order gumbo out or have someone named Hebert prepare it. Gumbo can be seafood gumbo or chicken and andouille gumbo or just about any indigenous ingredient, and all you need with it for a complete meal is

French bread. The important thing to remember is that you must have some each week or you may become sterile. The best gumbo at the right price is to be found at:

Bozo's 3117 21st St. in Metairie (831-8666)

Eddie's 2119 Law in Gentilly (945-2207)

Gumbo Shop 630 St. Peter in the Quarter (525-1486)

Acme Oyster House 724 Iberville in the Quarter (522-5973)

Dooky Chase's 2301 Orleans (821-0600)

Franky & Johnny's 321 Arabella (899-9146)

Mena's 622 Iberville (525-0217)

Eat 'Em Raw and Suck da Haids

Where to get raw and boiled seafood:

OYSTERS ON THE HALF-SHELL (highly recommended)

Acme Oyster House 724 Iberville in the French Quarter (522-5973)

Felix's 739 Iberville (522-4440)

Bozo's 3117 21st St. in Metairie, by Lakeside (831-8666)

Landry's 789 Harrison (Lakeview) (488-6496)

Messina's 2727 Williams in Kenner (469-7373)

The Pearl 119 St. Charles in the Central Business District (525-2901)

Bart's 8000 Lakeshore Dr. on the lake (282-0271)

DON'T DRINK THE WATER

According to the Environmental Protection Agency and local university research, the drinking water in New Orleans contains over 40 carcinogens after it is "purified," and is therefore unfit for human consumption. The tremendous amount of chlorine used to cleanse the Mississippi River water is also harmful. Nonetheless, it has won tasting competitions. We recommend drinking bottled spring water: Kentwood, Ozone, or Abita Springs.

Casamento's 4330 Magazine (895-9761)

R&O 210 Old Hammond Hwy. in Bucktown (831-1248)

Deanie's 1713 Lake in Bucktown (831-4141)

Cooter Brown's 509 S. Carrollton (866-9104)

Uglesich's 1238 Baronne St. (523-8571)

BOILED CRAWFISH, CRABS, AND SHRIMP

Most of the aforementioned oyster bars and restaurants also serve boiled seafood. Here are additional suggestions for boiled seafood only:

Pat Gillen's 1715 Jefferson Hwy. (834-1656)

Jaeger's 1701 Elysian Fields (947-0111)

Sid-Mar's 1824 Orpheum in Bucktown (831-9541)

Fitzgerald's West End (282-9254)

Bruning's West End (282-9395)

Several dozen other restaurants and bars excel at boiled seafood if you hit them at the right time!

Burgers—The Real Thing!

Bud's Broiler Locations around the city, but our favorite is by the tracks at 500 City Park Ave. (486-2559)

Camellia Grill 626 S. Carrollton (866-9573) The lost art of the diner hamburger lives on in grand fashion. The show alone is worth the cost of the burger.

Port of Call 838 Esplanade near the Faubourg (Faubourg Marigny) and the Quarter (523-0120) This is a real hideaway where the best burgers in town are served with baked potatoes!

Snug Harbor 626 Frenchmen in the Faubourg (949-0696) Wonderful burgers, hot jazz, and good prices.

Ted's Frostop 2900 Canal St./6303 S. Claiborne (821-3133) The original Lot-o-Burger recipe created in the fifties.

Lakeview Harbor 911 Harrison Ave. (486-4887) Burgers in the style of Port of Call and Snug Harbor.

Health-Food Restaurants

New Orleans' well-seasoned cuisine tends to be high in calories, cholesterol, and salt, so it's possible that you may want to take a break and hit the sprouts and other rabbit food periodically. We personally advise that you exercise regularly, don't drink the water, practice safe sex, and eat whatever you want. But if it's health food you must have, these establishments are quite wonderful and provide an imaginative selection that will appeal to even the least health conscious:

All Natural Foods Deli 5517 Magazine (891-2651) Features organic produce, tofu burgers, and vegetarian sushi.

Whole Foods Deli 3135 Esplanade (943-1626) Originally only a natural-foods grocery, Whole Foods has blossomed over the years as a well-regarded deli in its own right. You'll be surprised at creations that come out of this institution that draws folks from all over town.

East African Harvest 1643 Gentilly Blvd. (by the fairgrounds) (943-0787) This establishment has developed quite a reputation in a short period of time for surprisingly scrumptious meatless entrées.

NATURAL FOODS

Purchase your sprouts, grains, meats raised without steroids, and other health/organic items at the following locations:

Whole Foods Market 3135 Esplanade (943-1626)
Eve's Market 7700 Cohn St. (861-1626)

The Hottest Hobby

Collecting our local hot sauces could well be the ideal hobby. It's inexpensive, requires very little time, and it's clean as well as practical. It also provides a lazy susan laden with conversation pieces. Louisiana produces the greatest quality and quantity of hot sauces in the world. For less than $5 you can begin your collection with six to eight exciting varieties. Yes, they are like fine wines (okay, fine beers, and you had better have something cold handy). Actually, each hot sauce possesses its own distinctive taste, character, and, of course, inferno level.

BEST LOUISIANA HOT SAUCES
   Crystal Hot Sauce (red)
   McIlhenny Tabasco Pepper Sauce (red)
   Original Louisiana Hot Sauce (red)
   Trappey's Sauces (assorted)
   Louisiana Gold Pepper Sauce (red)
   Cajun Chef Green Hot Sauce (green)

MOST OFFERINGS
   Schwegmann's Grocery (various locations)
   Dorignac's Grocery (834-8216)
   Progress Grocery (525-6627)
   Central Grocery (523-1620)
   Louisiana Products on Jackson Square

Think Snow

Don' nobody know nothin' 'bout summer in the city till he spends a summer in the great Southern steam bath of New Orleans. A favorite method of tempering the heat and humidity is with a snowball. While we're certain they must exist in other places, snowball stands are ubiquitous in New Orleans. Everyone knows some entrepreneurial type who has ventured forth into the simmering streets to make his fortune in crushed ice and sweet syrups. The return trip is usually made with crushed hopes and a bitter memory of those barbarians who can't appreciate the delights of a nectar snowball with condensed milk.

The crème de la crème of New Orleans snowballs is not a snowball at all. It is a Sno-Bliz, and can only be found at one place in the world: **Hansen's Sno-Bliz**, at 4801 Tchoupitoulas (at Bordeaux Street). Mr. Hansen invented the Sno-Bliz machine, and he and his wife have operated their business since 1939. Sizes range from a small Bliz to a 30-gallon garbage can called "The Party Bliz."

Their motto is "there are no shortcuts to quality," and they stick to it religiously, with the results showing in their flavors (made fresh daily) and their clientele. Regular customers come from all over Louisiana and, according to their guest books, all over the world. In addition, they will pack these confections in dry ice to travel, and have shipped them to such exotic far-away lands as Dallas, Denver, and Sacramento.

Each year, the Hansens play host to field trips by elementary-school children and sorority, fraternity, and birthday parties. Hansen's is a local legend, and has been featured in all of New Orleans' media.

All it takes to establish a snowball business is a machine, a portable stand, a power supply, some flavored syrup, and miscellaneous paper products. For this reason, most of these business enterprises are fairly transient. However, two established longtime favorites are **Pandora's SnoWizard Snowball Shop** on North Carrollton at Dumaine near City Park, and **Williams** (or **Plum Street Snowball**) on Plum Street off South Carrollton.

Cocktail a la New Orleans

So you are sitting in the Napoleon House and the waiter comes up and asks, "May I bring you a cocktail?" The correct response is: "Yes, please bring me a _____."

Choose one:
  a) shrimp cocktail
  b) fruit cocktail
  c) Molotov cocktail
  d) Pimm's Cup

If you answered *d*, congratulations—you're no rube! If you answered any other letter, then read on, Dorothy, and take this newfound knowledge with you back to Kansas.

In the late 18th century a New Orleans pharmacist by the name of Peychaud concocted a tonic composed of bitters and Cognac. The receptacle for this clever potion was called a *coquetier*. Since French is mostly Greek to Americans, it quickly became known as a "cocktail." And so the alcoholic drink we know as the cocktail had its origins way down yonder in the

400 block of Royal Street in the French Quarter. Since that time the following cocktails and related beverages have been produced here:

Pimm's Cup Order this at the Napoleon House and get a souvenir glass. Garnished with a cucumber.

Hurricane There are many imitations of this most popular tourist drink, but Pat O'Brien's in the Quarter is the Real McCoy. Rum, fruit juices, and secret stuff in a souvenir glass.

Ramos Gin Fizz The Fairmont Hotel originated this gin and milk drink, which has other mysterious ingredients like egg whites and orange flower water to make it rich and exotic.

Sazerac Bourbon and bitters with sugar in a glass coated with Pernod. Sort of a licorice old-fashioned. Another original of the Fairmont.

Café Brûlot Made by mixing coffee with a potpourri of Cognac, cloves, cinnamon, and sugar that is ignited prior to combining with the coffee. Best as an after-dinner indulgence.

K-PAUL'S

Paul Prudhomme is New Orleans' world-renowned Cajun chef and the man who single-handedly made the redfish an endangered species. Even those on a moderate budget want to eat at the famous K-Paul's Kitchen. In our first edition (circa 1981), we recommended K-Paul's as having excellent Cajun food (it still does), with dinners starting at $6. Oh, for days gone by. With the passage of time everything has gotten more expensive. Unfortunately, the prices at K-Paul's have outpaced the inflation index many times over. We recommend buying his cookbook, Paul Prudhomme's Louisiana Kitchen. *At about $20, it's less than the price of one entrée at his restaurant. We also advise you cut his cayenne pepper in half to get a spicy dish that allows you to taste the other ingredients.*

Peychaud Bitters Named after you-know-who, and the special ingredient for several popular cocktails, including the old-fashioned.

Dixie Beer So? We know it's not a cocktail, but it is the last brewery left in New Orleans, struggling against the big, bad, Yankee breweries from Milwaukee, Chicago, and St. Louis.

Abita Beer A microbrewery from across the lake produces this excellent brew from pure artesian well water. Golden is closest to a traditional American beer. Amber is darker and Turbodog is heavier still. Your friends will be awed by your virility when they hear you're drinking a Turbodog. You ladies . . . hey, you'll like it too.

New Orleans Brunch

You can enjoy a New Orleans breakfast/brunch in the French Quarter for a fraction of what you pay at Brennan's and Commander's Palace. **Petunia's**, at 817 St. Louis (522-6440), serves Cajun and Creole specialties until midafternoon. Sure it's a little more expensive than our other recommended breakfast spots, but if you want to splurge a bit, but not too much, you'll want to venture here. Menu items include:

Pain Perdu, or "Lost Bread," which is the New Orleans version of French toast, using French bread

Grillades and Grits, a specially seasoned smothered steak with grits

Eggs Benedict, Eggs St. Louis, and **Eggs Melanza**

Cajun Sausage Breakfast (with grilled andouille and boudin sausages)

Breakfast at Tally Ho

You can bet that Audrey Hepburn never ate at Tally Ho because it's a long way from Tiffany's. But we'll take Tally Ho any day! The breakfasts are inexpensive and substantial, and you can't beat the French Quarter location (400 Chartres St., 566-7071). Our other recommended breakfast spots are:

Hummingbird 804 St. Charles Ave. (523-9165) The Hummingbird is a beehive of activity at any time of the day. The breakfasts are hearty, cheap, and delicious. Don't be afraid to enter, because you will find New Orleans' finest men in blue dining here at all hours. This place is an oasis on skid row, but we've seen formally attired ballgoers here at 4 A.M. Open 24 hours.

Camellia Grill 626 S. Carrollton Ave. at the river (866-9573) Possibly the best omelets in the city and by far the best showmanship of preparation. In the finest diner tradition. Camellia Grill is in a category by itself.

Ted's Frostop 2900 Canal St. and 6303 S. Claiborne (821-3133/861-3615) A family of five can eat a Ted's Frostop breakfast for just a few bucks. Ted's Frostop is a New Orleans tradition that dates back to the very first fast-food restaurants in the fifties.

Popeyes If your kids just insist on a glossy neon chain restaurant for breakfast, then bypass the golden arches and head for Popeyes, offering the best sausage biscuits in the land of mass advertising. Locations throughout the city.

Mother's 401 Poydras (Central Business District) (523-9656)

Rick's Famous Pancake Cottage 2547 Canal St. (Mid-City) (822-2630)

Rocky & Carlo's 613 W. St. Bernard Hwy. (Chalmette) (279-8323)

The Pearl 119 St. Charles (Downtown) (525-2901)

Russell's Marina Grill 8555 Pontchartrain (West End) (282-9980)

TIPPING

An enormous number of New Orleanians make their livings serving you in the city's many restaurants and bars. Please keep this in mind come tipping time, and leave them with a good impression of the fine folks from Live Oak or Starkville or wherever. Less than 15 percent is a serious faux pas; at least 20 percent should be rendered if the service is good.

Bagels, Beignets, and Croissants

New Orleans offers a fantastic array of new and historic spots where you can buy baked goods for light breakfasts. The only problem facing you is preventing the light breakfast from becoming a pastry overdose. Betcha can't eat just one!

Cafe du Monde in the French Quarter at Jackson Square (525-4544) The classic location for beignets (pronounced *ben-yays*—puffy, fried, rectangular doughnuts sprinkled with powdered sugar) and café au lait (a Crescent City tradition for coffee lovers).

Morning Call by Lakeside Shopping Center in Metairie (885-4068) Brings back magical memories of its earlier Quarter location. A venerable meeting place, with beignets as tasty as ever.

Charlie's Delicatessen 515 Harrison Ave. in Lakeview (486-1766) The Big Apple deli in the Big Easy. Bagels, lox, and the best kosher foods.

La Madeleine 547 St. Ann in the Quarter (568-9950) Possibly the most popular bakery in town. Breads and pastries in the best European tradition, with American and French coffees and a nice selection of teas. Unlike at the "coffeehouses," refills are free. We've noticed many European visitors having coffee and baguettes with jam for breakfast, a substantial meal for about $2. A second location is at scenic St. Charles and Carrollton. As a matter of fact, that's where we wrote this entry (861-8661).

La Marquise 625 Chartres in the French Quarter (524-0420) Offers a Lucullan feast of croissants filled with cream, chocolate, and every imaginable fruit. Marie Antoinette would lose her head here for sure! Order a napoleon, as they are superior to any in the city.

Croissant D'Or 617 Ursulines in the old Angelo Brocato ice-cream parlor (524-4663) Another ethereal experience, both for its bakery delights and ambience of local flavor.

Martin Wine Cellar 3827 Baronne (899-7411) An example of Epicurean eclecticism. Martin has a little of everything—

fresh breads, cheeses, bagels, lox, wines, and sandwiches. It is a super deli and the #1 place for wine selection in New Orleans.

Cafe Pontchartrain 2031 St. Charles Ave. in the Pontchartrain Hotel (524-0581) An opportunity for you to see one of the city's grand hotels without paying the price. This is probably as close as you'll get to the famed and fabulous Pontchartrain Room, with its glorious Mile-High Pie and megaton bills, but you can sit and dream as you sample the Cafe's wonderful blueberry muffins.

Landry's 789 Harrison Ave. (488-6496) Among the least expensive in town. The friendly service adds to the morning pleasure.

Coffeehouses

In the early 1980s, a coffeehouse opened on Maple Street in the University section of Uptown. Shortly thereafter, a couple more popped up around town. When there were about three of these establishments in town, most folks thought that the market was saturated.

In the mid-nineties, conventional wisdom of a decade earlier has been proven wrong—dreadfully wrong! Nowadays there seem to be at least three coffeehouses per block. Okay, you caught us exaggerating again. But there are a lot of 'em. After all, what better way to sit, think, converse, read, and engage in those pursuits that are not necessarily suited to our traditional gathering places, the barrooms?

As with bars and restaurants, the coffeehouses have distinct personalities. The suburbs have well-lit shops tucked away in strip malls that cater to yuppie moms, business people, and the like. This is not to say that these establishments are unpleasant meeting points or have substandard fare. To the contrary, most are quite good and pleasant places to sit and chat if you're in the vicinity and are not particularly concerned about atmosphere.

Then there are what we'll call the in-betweeners, which have a pleasant, nonthreatening atmosphere with just a touch of funk.

The clientele spans the spectrum from students to professionals.

Then there are those from the mold of the prototype, Bohemian coffeehouse of the Kerouac, Ginsberg, Maynard G. Krebs era. When you're in this frame of mind, the others just won't do. It's not the coffee, the edibles, or the literature. It's the clientele and the mood.

In New Orleans we have two of these. **Kaldi's** is in the French Quarter on Decatur Street at the corner of St. Philip. The building itself has an illustrious history. In the late sixties, the Seven Seas and Bonaparte's Retreat on the adjacent corners were the hub of the hip community. The building that houses Kaldi's was called the Bank, a sometime live-music venue and full-time communal living quarters. Alas, the venerable old building was later transmogrified into a dispensary of pornographic literature and, to put it delicately, marital aids.

We are happy to report that the building has been resurrected in a manner appropriate to its history. Kaldi's is a refuge in the midst of the increasingly touristy Decatur Street. The Bohemian element is well represented and they don't come any funkier than the crowd at Kaldi's. One wonders where they come from and where they go to.

The neighborhood denizens sit for hours. You can read, play chess or backgammon, meditate, and devise your schemes to save Western civilization or take over small third world countries. More importantly, you can revel in the atmosphere.

CHEAP SOUVENIRS OF NEW ORLEANS

N.O. music from most record shops
C.D.M. (Cafe du Monde) or Luzianne coffee
A box of pralines
French Market beignet mix
A Pat O'Brien's Hurricane glass
A bag of red beans
Dixie and Abita beer
Hot sauce

Rue de la Course is located in the Lower Garden District at the corner of Race and Magazine streets. In an earlier era, Race Street was known as rue de la Course. The Lower Garden District is one of the city's oldest neighborhoods. The once grand homes have been through several cycles of disrepair and renovation. The neighborhood seems to be on the upswing or at least has settled into a harmonious mix of urban inhabitants. The rallying site for the neighborhood and way station for others from the outlying areas is Rue de la Course.

Rue de la Course fits the mold of what a coffeehouse should be. It is housed in the corner of a 19th-century commercial building. When years of "improvements" were stripped away, the original, pressed-tin ceiling was found to be intact. This is not some space that has been outfitted with stained glass, ferns, and brass rails to create the appearance of character. This is the real thing. It's old, it's genuine, and it exudes character. Hang out; it's good for the soul. The coffee, in all its variations, is good too.

Kaldi's 941 Decatur (586-8989)

Rue de la Course 1500 Magazine (529-1455)

Orleans Coffee Exchange 712 Orleans Ave. (522-5710) Wholesale coffee beans. This tiny shop roasts its own.

P.J.'s 7624 Maple (866-9963), 5432 Magazine, 637 N. Carrollton, 634 Frenchmen, and 2727 Prytania (tell Kathy Redmann *Half-Shell* sent you)

Plantation Coffeehouse 5555 Canal Blvd. (482-3164)

True Brew 3133 Ponce de Leon (947-3948), and 200 Julia St. (524-8441)

FRENCH MARKET

One of the principal open-air attractions of the French Quarter, the French Market extends along Decatur and North Peters streets, offering fresh produce, such as Creole tomatoes, mirlitons, pecans, Louisiana squash, and watermelons, as well as all other standard market fare. Great idea for budget meals!

Croissant D'Or 617 Ursulines St. (524-4663)

La Madeleine 547 St. Ann (568-9950), and 601 S. Carrollton (861-8661) A café and bakery as well as a coffeehouse. If you're just going for coffee, pastry, and conversation, avoid the breakfast and lunch crowds. Coffee refills are free.

Angelo Brocato's 214 N. Carrollton near City Park (486-0078), and 537 St. Ann St. at Jackson Square (525-9676) Doesn't exactly fit the coffeehouse mold, but they do have coffee, espresso, and cappuccino. They also have cakes, pastries, and ice cream, including their own Italian delicacies such as cannoli, Italian fig cookies, and lemon and strawberry ice.

The Neutral Ground 5110 Danneel St. (891-3381) A coffeehouse and the local hot spot for folk and bluegrass music. On any given night there is a lineup of several acts to entertain the patrons. If you want to play music, sign up in advance. If you want to listen to music, play chess, or mingle, show up and stake your claim to a corner of a couch. No cover charge, but contribute what you can when the hat is passed. No alcohol is served, so you can even take the kids.

City Park Cafe 520 City Park Ave. Across from Delgado Community College, this coffeehouse is on the site of the old Avenue Po' Boys, established in 1931. Howard Hens (whose family owned the Avenue) and Mary Anne McKearan keep the tradition alive.

Music and Night Life

Ernie K-Doe, née Kador, that colorful character who sang about his mother-in-law, was the first to advance the idea when he speculated that all music originated in New Orleans. One can imagine some prehistoric swamp dweller picking up a bone and expressing himself by beating out a rhythm on a hollow log. Others no doubt heard, began their own percussion ensembles, and the beat emanated across the countryside. A few thousand years later, slaves were gathering in Congo Square, the site of the Municipal Auditorium off of Rampart Street, to celebrate time off with dance and rhythm. In the early part of the 20th century, New Orleans exported musicians to the rest of the country with a style of music labeled "jazz."

During the late fifties and early sixties, our contribution to the world music scene was the rhythm and blues seed of the genre that came to be known as rock 'n' roll. The previous paragraph may have been a work of fiction, but even if Bill Haley and the Comets are recognized as the founding fathers of rock, no one can dispute the contribution of Fats Domino, a native son, Little Richard, who made his first recording here, and the more obscure local hero, Henry Roeland Byrd, known professionally as Professor Longhair. Cosimo Matassa's recording studio in the 800 block of Camp Street turned out a string of hits in the late fifties and early sixties. Names such as Frankie Ford ("Sea Cruise"), Shirley and Lee ("Let the Good Times Roll"), and the Dixie Cups ("Chapel of Love") were common in the country's top-40 play lists.

After the initial excitement died down, an occasional New Orleans hit would wend its way into the nation's airwaves. Aaron Neville's "Tell It Like It Is" made a big splash about the time brother Art was funking it up with the Meters. Mac Rebennack became Dr. John the "Night Tripper" and released his *Gris Gris* album with the voodoo chant of "Walk on Gilded

Splinters," still a New Orleans favorite. It's a Beautiful Day came to town in the early seventies and left with one of our top guitar players, Billy Gregory.

The seventies and eighties were relatively quiet as far as New Orleans' contributions to the radio are concerned. Locally, the Rhapsodizers and Little Queenie and the Percolators were heating up the club scene along with some of those outlaw-influenced country bands like the Copas Brothers, Road Apple, and Kurt Kasson and the Wheeler Sisters.

Ed Voelker and Frank Bua of the Rhapsodizers joined with Dave Malone and Reggie Scanlan of Road Apple to form the quintessential party band, the Radiators. John Magnie and Tommy Malone left the Percolators to create the Continental Drifters and ultimately the subdudes (yes, with a small *s*).

Riding the New Wave into the early eighties, the Cold created a phenomenon and disappeared faster than you could sing "Three Chord City." The Normals and the Red Rockers both contained talent destined to shape the musical future of the nineties.

The Nevilles are still the first family of New Orleans funk with the Marsalises laying claim to the realm of jazz. The Radiators are still fixtures on the party scene and have achieved legendary status.

But the times they are a-changing . . . for the better. There has not only been an influx of talent who feels that this is the proper environment in which to create, but a new generation of homegrown talent has exploded on the scene. There is so much good music to be heard on any given night that it is impossible to name everyone worthy of recognition. Follow our suggestions for names and places and you will rarely be disappointed.

The Nevilles "Tell It Like It Is"!

The Neville family has been a part of the local and national music scene since the late fifties. Art Neville was a member of the Meters, who received national airplay in the late sixties with "Cissy Strut" and "Sophisticated Cissy." In the mid-seventies the group recorded a New Orleans classic, "They All Axed for You." Art was also a member of the Hawkettes, who recorded "Mardi Gras Mambo," one of a select group of Mardi Gras anthems resurrected each year at carnival time. Brother Aaron is probably the most recognizable name in the family, due to his monster hit, "Tell It Like It Is," and the Grammy Award-winning duet with Linda Ronstadt, "Don't Know Much."

At the end of the seventies, Art and Aaron joined forces with brothers Charles and Cyril to form the Neville Brothers Band. Since that time, the band has recorded several albums and toured extensively, opening for such notables as the Rolling Stones. The Neville Brothers' fame and musical reputation grows with each passing year.

The Neville Brothers' offspring are also making their musical mark in the world. Aaron's son Ivan is making a name for himself on the national music scene, and Charles' daughter Charmaine fronts a loosely knit organization known as Charmaine Neville and Friends. Charmaine is without question the finest female vocalist in New Orleans, and that is not a statement to be made lightly. If jazz and R&B suit your musical tastes, a Charmaine Neville performance should be high on your list of must-sees.

Allen Toussaint

The undisputed genius behind the sound that became identified with New Orleans rhythm and blues is Allen Toussaint.

NAME THAT TUNE

Many of the musicians who had hits back when the New Orleans R&B sound dominated the airwaves are still around and performing. Lest we forget their claim to fame, many are identified by the unique practice of using the name of the respective hit song as the artist's middle name. Among the notables are Oliver ("Who Shot the LaLa?") Morgan, Jesse ("Ooh Poo Pah Doo") Hill, and Earl ("Trick Bag") King.

He wrote the majority of the hits that came out of the Crescent City from the late fifties to the seventies and served as producer on many others. Several of Allen's tunes were written under the pseudonym of Naomi Neville.

Allen is a regular at the Jazz Fest and occasionally performs around town. Usually dressed in a silver lamé tuxedo and sandals, he also performs with his New Orleans Rhythm and Blues Revue. He plays a set of his own songs and then backs up a parade of New Orleans musical legends. If you have the opportunity, this show should not be missed for *any* reason. Here is a random sampling of Toussaint compositions:

"A Certain Girl" performed by Ernie K-Doe
"Fortune Teller" performed by Bennie Spellman
"I Like It Like That" performed by Chris Kenner
"Over You" performed by Aaron Neville
"All These Things" performed by Art Neville
"It's Raining" performed by Irma Thomas
"Southern Nights" performed by Glen Campbell
"Java" performed by Al Hirt
"Whipped Cream" performed by Herb Alpert
"Sneaking Sally Through the Alley" performed by Lee Dorsey/Robert Palmer

Danny Barker

Danny Barker, the dean of New Orleans jazz musicians, passed away in 1994. He was such a vital part of jazz history that this entry remains as a tribute. He played with all the legendary musicians and probably taught them a thing or two. He was also a noted jazz historian and storyteller, acquiring much of his knowledge through personal experience. His wife, "Blue" Lu, is an accomplished composer who acquired the name from her risqué lyrics. Maria Muldaur did Lu's song "Don't You Feel My Leg" on her *Midnight at the Oasis* album.

The Radiators

New Orleans' most recent contribution to the national music scene is the Radiators, or simply, "Da Rads," as they're known locally. A performance by the Radiators is guaranteed to coax the crazies from the closets, and the dancing crowd is usually as much of an attraction as the music. The group has recorded several albums. The earliest, recorded live at Tipitina's at the band's own expense, is on the Croaker label. These early recordings are classic Radiators performances. Since many insist that music must be categorized, the music of the Radiators is called "Fish Head" music, because there's nothing funkier than a fish head.

Irma Thomas

In 1989, Irma Thomas was officially recognized as New Orleans' First Lady of Music. She began recording as a teen in the late fifties and is still looking and sounding great.

Bobby Cure and the Summertime Blues

It's a shame that the great top-40 rock 'n' roll songs of the sixties are now referred to as "oldies," but their timeless quality accounts for their popularity in the waning years of the century. Bobby Cure and the Summertime Blues are always playing somewhere, and their renditions of that old-time rock 'n' roll never fail to provide a good time. Bobby is the lead vocalist and handles the repartee, but when Robin steps up to the microphone and belts out a Dusty Springfield number, she'll tear your heart out.

The Continental Drifters

Those of you who have heard of Peter Holsapple would associate the name with the Db's, REM, and the early-eighties Athens, Ga., music scene. Well, Peter met up with a couple of New Orleanians, Ray Ganucheau and Carlo Nuccio, who had been in the successor band to Little Queenie and the Percolators, the Continental Drifters. When the original members drifted apart, Ganucheau kept the name and along with Holsapple and Nuccio formed the nucleus of one of the most creative and original musical collaborations to grace the local stages in years.

Those three, however, do not tell the whole story. Holsapple's wife, Susan Cowsill, is also a player. You may remember the Cowsills' megahits from the sixties, "The Rain, the Park, and Other Things" and "Hair." If you've really got a head full of trivia, you may remember the more obscure follow-up, "Indian Lake." Susan was the youngest member of the clan. And then there's former Bangle Vickie Peterson—remember, early eighties MTV, "Walk Like an Egyptian" and "Manic Monday"? Now she is singing and playing guitar with the Drifters. All the members are songwriters and share vocal duties. They don't play often but if you have the opportunity to attend a show, don't miss it.

The subdudes

As noted earlier, John Magnie and Tommy Malone of the subdudes are veterans of the New Orleans music scene. Both were members of the legendary Little Queenie and the Percolators. After a short stint with Johnny Ray Allen as the Continental Drifters, they recruited the services of Steve Amadee and relocated to Magnie's native Colorado. It turned out to be the right place at the right time to perfect the sound. Three CDs later, the venture has proved to be successful.

Allen and Malone have relocated to southeast Louisiana, with Magnie and Amadee putting down roots in Colorado. Nonetheless, the group comes together for many local appearances. These guys should be on your "must see" list.

Anders Osborne and Teresa Andersson

Anders is a Swedish import whose musical style, reminiscent of Little Feat, is a New Orleans natural. His companion, Teresa Andersson, also sings with his group but is at her best on her own. She is an accomplished jazz vocalist reminiscent of Rickie Lee Jones, with a knack for making the jazz standards fresh again.

Dash Rip Rock

One hesitates to use the musical cliché "high energy," but in the case of Dash Rip Rock, that about sums it up. This trio is a favorite in the local clubs with their onstage leaps and antics and their clever musical parodies. The band also has a repertoire of originals that are represented on their three recordings of good, listenable, danceable rock 'n' roll.

Cowboy Mouth

Fred LeBlanc was the drummer for Dash Rip Rock. John Thomas Griffith has been a Red Rocker, a solo artist, and half of a duo. Steve Walters was a Normal and Paul Sanchez, a singer-songwriter. Together, these guys generate excitement and a lot of good rock 'n' roll as Cowboy Mouth. Griffith, Sanchez, and Walters, the axe men, are first-rate instrumentalists and songwriters and are fairly active on stage—pacing, climbing, and jumping. Fred is the drummer and primary vocalist but is not your usual percussionist tucked away at the back of the stage. His drums are parked front and center as he brutally flails away. This is what Keith Moon would have been if the Who had ever let him out from the back of the stage. LeBlanc glares and grimaces like a madman, but when he opens his mouth to sing, the rich baritone tempers the crazed persona. It is difficult to fathom how this voice can dwell within that savage exterior.

Seek out a live performance and request "Another Cup of Coffee" or "Any Little Bit." Then, head straight to a local record shop and pick up a CD to take home. With a little Word of Mouth, these guys may be appearing in your hometown.

As if being part of a rock band on the brink of stardom were not enough, the Cowboys do some moonlighting. John is a member of a neotraditional country and western band, the Wild Peyotes. Fred and Paul make solo acoustic appearances. Paul performs his own compositions; Fred performs his own songs along with covers of tunes like Clarence Carter's "Slip Away" and "Gypsies, Tramps, and Thieves." You were, of course, hoping you'd never hear that song again. When Fred does it, you'll forget you ever heard the schlock by the tattooed lady.

J. Monque'D Blues Band

When this wild man (whose name is pronounced "Jay Monkey Dee") shouts, "I am the blues!" you have no reason to doubt his audacity or veracity.

Bryan Lee

A French Quarter fixture, this blind guitarist/singer was born to play the blues. Backed by the Jump Street Five.

Walter ("Wolfman") Washington and the Roadmasters

Walter has been part of the New Orleans music scene for many, many years and has played with all the legends. He got his nickname from his missing front teeth, which made his canines appear more prominent than normal. His new dentures haven't hindered his music. He equals or surpasses the more famous names of the blues genre.

John Mooney

While we're talking blues, we can't overlook John Mooney. He plays with his band, Bluesiana, and often appears solo on Sunday nights.

The Iguanas

Tex-Mex and R&B might seem like an unlikely combination until you hear the Iguanas mix it up. Jimmy Buffett heard them and signed them to his Margaritaville label. CDs available.

Noble Coyotes

You'll find this tight, talented group playing its danceable brand of blues at various roadhouse-type bars around the city. Fronted by Mitch Bancroft on harmonica/vocals and Dmitri Resnik on guitar, this foursome will put you in mind of the Fabulous Thunderbirds, but if you're not a fan of the latter, go anyway. The Coyotes are pure fun, and are sure to please blues lovers of all kinds.

Irene and the Mikes

The nucleus of this sixties throwback is Irene the singer and her sidekick, Mike the guitar player. At one point, all the sidemen as well as the sound man were named Mike.

Luther Kent

Luther, a big man with a big voice and a former member of Blood, Sweat & Tears, usually has an excellent horn section. At the '94 Jazz Fest he assembled a horn section of 10 (*10!*). Is it necessary to tell you the crowd was blown away?

Sunpie and the Louisiana Sunspots

Sunpie (Bruce Barnes) is a park ranger during the day and a musician by night. Zydeco and blues.

Kermit Ruffins

Kermit and the Rebirth Brass Band began playing second-line jazz on French Quarter street corners as children. When we say children, we are talking 10 to 12 years old. Kermit still plays with the Rebirth on occasion but has become a celebrity in his own right, the heir apparent to Louis Armstrong.

Others Worthy of Your Time and Money

The Bingemen Rock

The Bagdaddies Rock

Dead Eye Dick Modern rock

Lump Rock/jazz but not jazz rock

Big Sun Rock

Galactic We used to call it soul music when Otis Redding and Sam and Dave played it. Today it's referred to as funk.

Reliable Sources

This is a non-exhaustive list of the great music you can hear on any given night that you happen to be in New Orleans. To find out who is playing where, pick up a copy of *Offbeat* magazine free at most local record stores. Keith Spera, the editor and "Dis 'n' Dat" columnist, will keep you in tune with the who, where, and when of the local music scene.

Scott Aiges is the music writer for *The Times-Picayune.* The Friday Lagniappe tabloid is his primary outlet. Scott has an uncanny knack for putting labels on music and musicians in such a way that even the most out of touch can figure out what's going on.

John Sinclair is a disc jockey at WWOZ-FM, a musicologist, an *Offbeat* columnist, and a poet. He achieved notoriety in the sixties for his politically radical views and as the manager of the militant rock band the MC5. Kick out the jams, brothers and sisters.

Robert Palmer, not the one who is "simply irresistible" but the former writer for *Rolling Stone,* was documenting traditional blues in the Mississippi Delta and decided New Orleans was the proper incubator for his muses. He can be found haunting the Treme music scene (just above the French Quarter).

Traditional Jazz, Dixieland, and the Brass Bands

This is the music that New Orleans is most famous for, and it is therefore the easiest to find. Everybody gets to Bourbon Street, and Bourbon Street is still the place where it's at, as we say. Usually the music filters into the streets and provides accompaniment for the tap-dancing kids with bottle caps nailed to the bottom of their Keds—nobody is going to put nails in their Air Jordans!

STREET MUSICIANS

New Orleans is one of the few cities in the United States where musicians and entertainers may legally perform on the streets for donations. During the day, try Royal Street in the French Quarter or Jackson Square for a minstrel performance. Most street musicians perform in order to eat, so don't forget to drop a couple of coins into the empty guitar case or hat!

Remember, however, Bourbon Street exists off tourist dollars, and you will spend many of them in the Bourbon Street clubs. Even if there is no admission there will be a minimum drink order. This means you must buy at least one and frequently two drinks per hour set of music. These drinks are often very small and expensive, and don't think you'll get off easy by ordering a cola.

On Bourbon Street, the Famous Door has been a Dixieland hot spot since time began. Maison Bourbon, at the corner of St. Peter, usually has its doors open for all to hear the music, which starts in the early afternoon and goes well into the night.

Names to look for in the Dixieland and brass band tradition other than those already mentioned include: the Olympia Brass Band, the Original Tuxedo Jazz Band, the Original Crescent City Jazz Band and, when they are not on tour, the Dirty Dozen Brass Band and the Rebirth Brass Band. You may have to look beyond Bourbon Street and its standard fare for talent of this caliber.

Progressive Jazz

Progressive jazz is thriving in New Orleans! There exists a creative and talented community of musicians, and the interaction of the various artists and groups will provide the jazz aficionado with an endless variety of excellent progressive jazz.

JAZZ FUNERALS

The jazz funeral is a custom peculiar to New Orleans. When a musician dies, a brass band will join the funeral procession. The band usually plays hymns on the way to the gravesite. On the return trip the music is much livelier, and the procession turns into a parade. The dancers behind the band form what is called a "second line," which grows as passersby join in the dancing. In present times the band may not actually march to the gravesite, but it usually does stage a parade in the neighborhood. An altogether fitting way to go! Unfortunately, jazz funerals occur much too often.

The jazz community in New Orleans is structured around several established groups and many individual musicians. On any given night one can find at least one of the well-known groups playing or a gathering of solo artists jamming in local clubs. Some of the names to look for include: Tony Dagradi, Steve Masakowski, John Vidacovich, James Rivers, Red Tyler, David Torkanowsky, Nicholas Payton, Jim Singleton, Scott Sanders, and Olivier Bou. These musicians may be with their regular groups, such as Dagradi's Astral Project, Masakowski's Mars, and Woodenhead, or they may interact in an endless array of combinations. Take them as you find them, and enjoy.

Record Stores

The national chains have moved in to dominate the new record/CD/cassette market, but there are still several locally owned shops that offer used and rare recorded music.

Record Ron 1129 Decatur St. (524-9444), and 239 Chartres (522-2239) Another one of those Quarter dwellers who has been around through many phases of what is hip and trendy. Ron began selling his used records at the flea market on weekends and eventually opened a small shop on Decatur Street. These shops are a mother lode of "vintage vinyl," as they say on the radio. Ron has become a semicelebrity in recent years due to his advertisements announcing his special sales, such as his annual event chronicling his divorce. His slogan is "tell me I sent you." Check out Record Ron's stuff at 239 Chartres. Ron has accumulated a fascinating array of sixties memorabilia. Get your lava lamps and lunch boxes here.

Jim Russell Records 1837 Magazine St. (522-2602) The undisputed champion in the longevity department.

Gold Mine Rare Records and Cards 4222 Magazine St. (899-6905) This has been around for quite a while also.

Sounds Familiar 829 Chartres St. (523-8249) Extensive jazz selection.

Rock N Roll Records and Collectibles 1214 Decatur (561-5683) As the name implies, records and artifacts of bygone musical eras.

The Louisiana Music Factory 225 N. Peters (523-1094) The best selection of New Orleans and Louisiana music can be found here. CDs, cassettes, vinyl, books, posters, and the most complete selection of T-shirts in town. Many local groups play free concerts here to introduce their new releases.

The Mushroom 1037 Broadway (866-6065) Originated as a record co-op on the Tulane campus back in the late sixties. It's still around and carries the best selection of Grateful Dead items that these old hippies have ever seen.

Tower Records 408 N. Peters in the Jax Brewery (529-4411) Sometimes you have to go to one of those big chain stores to get what you want. If you must, then we recommend Tower. Park in the lot. One hour is free.

Memory Lane Records 6417 Airline Hwy. in the Airline Highway Shopping Center (733-2120) Has been around since 1970 and offers 15,000 45s from the fifties and sixties that are brand new.

Instruments

International Vintage Guitars 1011 Magazine St. (524-4557) If you want to create music—not just listen to it—check out the instruments here.

That's Trash, That's Cool 3117 Magazine (891-COOL)— that's the name of the shop—also has a selection of Telecasters, Les Pauls, and the mighty Super Reverbs.

Rock-N-Roll Music Inc. 4805 Baudin (486-7625) This old motorcycle warehouse in Mid-City near I-10 has long served the local music community with new and used guitar equipment.

Musical Research

For those who approach music from a scholarly standpoint, there are many resources in New Orleans to facilitate your musical research.

Howard-Tilton Library (865-5688) This library at Tulane University houses the William Ranson Hogan Jazz Archives. This is an extensive collection of recorded music, historical photographs, and, of course, books and documents. The curator, Bruce Raeburn, has played drums through many musical trends. He didn't have to keep his day job.

The Louisiana State Museum old U.S. Mint on Esplanade at Decatur (568-6975) A collection to rival that of Tulane. In addition, there is a display of musical instruments played by some of the New Orleans greats.

Loyola University Music Library 6363 St. Charles Ave. (865-2774) A huge collection of music by Louisiana artists, encompassing every musical persuasion.

The Historic New Orleans Collection 533 Royal St. (523-4662) Sheet music, photographs, manuscripts, and recordings.

Music Clubs

One of the main attractions for visitors to New Orleans is the music. After all, the city is known as the birthplace of jazz. We also possess a rich heritage of rhythm and blues, which dominated the American rock scene in the late fifties and early sixties. Both of these indigenous forms are easily accessible to the visitor who knows where to locate them. Additionally, there are many clubs and bars where one can hear just about any other type of music desired.

The following guide to local music clubs is guaranteed to have something to please everyone.

Highlight: Rock 'n' Bowl

Most cities have their share of music clubs and New Orleans is blessed with a multitude of live-music outlets, some of which, like Tipitina's, have achieved legendary status. On any given night there is a variety of live music to satisfy the most eclectic tastes.

The most unique and easily the most comfortable of the local venues is Rock 'n' Bowl, officially known as Mid-City Bowling Lanes. As the name implies, you can rock to the best bands the region has to offer, and you can bowl. That's right, bowl, just like Ralph Kramden and Ed Norton used to do. This may seem like a peculiar combination to some folks, but not to the locals who flock to the RnB to listen, dance, and bowl.

In 1988, John Blancher took over a nearly defunct bowling alley in a part of town where no one really wanted to go. The previous owners, the Knights of Columbus, no doubt heaved a major sigh of relief when they saw John coming.

The theater crowd found it first and there were tales of dancing on the tables and ball racks. Those were the days when there was only a jukebox to provide the stimulus. A year after he opened the doors, John decided that live music was the way to go. He has never looked back.

LEGENDS

Wanna talk to a legendary veteran of the New Orleans music scene? Stop by Matassa Grocery at 1001 Dauphine St. in the Quarter and ask for Cosimo. Cosimo Matassa owned the recording studio and served as producer on the majority of the R&B hits that defined the New Orleans sound in the early sixties.

Want more? Stop by the Pharmacy Museum on Royal Street and visit a while with Oliver ("Who Shot the LaLa?") Morgan. Oliver's hit will always be the question most often asked by inquiring minds in New Orleans.

Don't stop there. Drive by Fats Domino's house. Take Rampart away from Canal. Keep going as it turns into St. Claude Avenue at Esplanade. (Does anyone pray to St. Claude?) When you're deep in the Ninth Ward, turn left on Caffin Avenue and you're there. Believe us, you'll know.

Mid-City features live music four or five nights a week. The groups are the hottest in the area. Thursday has become zydeco night with Acadiana's best up and comers like Chubby Carrier Beau Jocque to the legendary Boozoo Chavis. (Boozoo, that's who!) The weekends can feature the likes of the Iguanas, who played their formative gigs here, to the revered New Orleans rhythm and blues artists like Johnny Adams, Snooks Eaglin, funk master George Porter, Jr., or J. Monque'D with his low-down blues.

So what is the attraction that compels Robert Plant and Mick Jagger to stop in when they're in town or Tom Cruise to reserve all the lanes for his entourage on Saturday night while he was here playing the Vampire Lestat? The charm is indefinable but the elements are apparent. John Blancher is as congenial a host as you would ever hope to encounter. He books the bands himself and the variety and quality of the music is above reproach. The decor is 1960s pink Brunswick bowling alley with molded plastic chairs.

The cover charges and drink prices are reasonable and could be considered bargains compared to most music clubs. The dancing is a hedonistic frenzy. Tables, ball racks, and on occasion even the bar have all served as go-go platforms.

If all of the above assets are not enough, there's one more overwhelming plus about Rock 'n' Bowl. The place is large enough and has enough ceiling fans to disperse the smoke generated by those who still don't have the self-discipline to shake the monkey. In most clubs, one can absorb enough secondhand

---

AL HIRT

Not enough is said about Al Hirt, who along with Patout's, Cajun Cabin, and Chris Owens is trying to preserve a corner of Bourbon Street and keep the T-shirt shops at bay. Al is still belting out talented blasts from his horn. His performance remains strong and New Orleans should be thankful for his promotion while on international tours.

smoke to grow a tumor. If your health is not seriously damaged, your pocket book will be when you have to pay the cleaners to fumigate the new spring ensemble. Mid-City is not smoke free; however, it is certainly the least offensive environment of all New Orleans music clubs.

While we can only enumerate the elements that comprise the whole, Blancher knows exactly why his place is a success. Even though he and his staff sing, "We built this city on Rock 'n' Bowl," John will tell you his good fortune is the result of divine providence, and he is serious. Rock 'n' Bowl is located at 4133 S. Carrollton Ave., near Tulane Avenue. (482-3133)

TIPITINA'S

The granddaddy of the New Orleans music clubs is the internationally known Tipitina's. Named after a song by the legendary Professor Longhair, the club was originally conceived as a venue for da Professa', or simply, "Fess," as he was known locally. Tip's opened in the mid-seventies, but fell on hard times in 1984 and closed for a while. In 1985, under new ownership, the club was remodeled and the tradition resumed. Now it's as if the club never missed a beat.

This is where you get the best music in the city. Local and national acts are here every night of the week playing every kind of music imaginable. One night you can hear the local progressive rock bands and the next night someone like King Sunny Ade from Nigeria, Doug Sahm, Dave Mason, or Hall and Oates shows up on stage. The Nevilles and the Radiators started out here and, along with Dr. John, always return when they are in town. Tipitina's is at 501 Napoleon at Tchoupitoulas. (897-3943)

THE UPTOWN CLUBS

If you're looking for live music, on any given night you can take the streetcar to Oak Street, walk two blocks toward the river, and you'll find it. The **Maple Leaf** is a venerable old dance hall that features a wide variety of music, and if you're looking for that New Orleans mystique, this is the place. The natives are here and always restless. The biggest night is

Thursday, when a Cajun band plays and the locals are in a two-stepping frenzy. Weekends usually find groups from outlying areas, and the music can run the gamut from reggae to rhythm and blues to some of the better known Cajun and zydeco bands. If you're looking for a literary way to spend a Sunday afternoon, check out the poetry readings by local and regional writers. The atmosphere at the Leaf is ultracasual, and the admission and drink prices are reasonable.

If you're still not satisfied, walk two blocks to Willow and Dante and you have two more choices. On the river side of Dante, across from the streetcar barn, is **Jimmy's Club**, probably (along with the Maple Leaf) one of the oldest music clubs in the city. Jimmy's features local and national acts of every description—progressive rock, heavy metal, rhythm and blues, rockabilly, and most anything else you can name.

On the downtown side of Dante is **Carrollton Station**. This is a neighborhood bar with a pleasant atmosphere and weekend music. Sunday nights feature acoustic sets by local talent such as Fred LeBlanc and Peter Holsapple.

Finally, out on River Road beyond the parish line is the **River Shack Tavern**—good atmosphere, good music, and some very tacky ashtrays.

Maple Leaf 8316 Oak St. (866-LEAF)

Jimmy's 8200 Willow St. (861-8200)

TICKETS, PLEASE

The absolute best kept New Orleans secret—and we'll probably be exiled for revealing this—is that WTUL gives away tickets to the Uptown nightclubs. Okay, skeptic, we know the commercial stations scream FREE TICKETS 24 hours a day, but the difference at 'TUL is that you can usually win some if you listen diligently for about an hour. We can guarantee that you will not read this in any other publication, not even those in-the-know weeklies or the hip monthlies.

Carrollton Station 8140 Willow St. (865-9190)

River Shack Tavern 3449 River Rd. (834-4938)

THE DOWNTOWN CLUBS

Tropical Isle 738 Toulouse St. (525-1689) Al Miller and his band, Late As Usual, are a fixture at this club. Modest cover on weekends. The Dungeon is still next door.

The Old Absinthe Bar 400 Bourbon St. (525-8108) There is a debate raging between patrons of the Old Absinthe House down the street and this late-night R&B palace as to which is the oldest, but that's for the barroom regulars to discuss over cocktails. When Bryan Lee and the Jump Street Five strike up the band, no one cares anyway.

Snug Harbor 626 Frenchmen St. (949-0696) The premier progressive jazz club in the city is Snug Harbor, and a snug harbor it truly is. All the New Orleans jazz greats play here regularly, and those who have gone on to national fame— like Harry Connick, Jr., the whole Marsalis family, Terence Blanchard, and Donald Harrison—started here and return on a regular basis.

Preservation Hall 726 St. Peter (523-8939) If you really want to hear traditional jazz, the place to go is Preservation Hall on St. Peter Street, next to Pat O'Brien's. The lines form early to hear the originals playing the purest form of the genre. Many Europeans are in attendance and consider a visit to Preservation Hall as a pilgrimage to Mecca.

Palm Court Jazz Cafe 1204 Decatur St. (525-0200) Down on Decatur Street, some former Atlantans who realized the folly of trying to preserve the heritage of traditional jazz in a city devoid of soul opened one of our town's truly unique institutions. The Palm Court Jazz Cafe is a place where you can peruse the extensive collection of jazz recordings and select your own background music to listen to while you dine. At night, live music by legendary musicians like Wendell Brunious, coupled with the pleasant atmosphere, makes the Palm Court a truly great place to hear traditional jazz. The GHB Foundation, upstairs, offers an extensive catalog of traditional jazz albums for sale and also serves as an information center for New Orleans music.

The House of Blues 225 Decatur St. (529-BLUE) The first time Isaac Tigrett came to town, he opened his Hard Rock Cafe, which added nothing to the ambience of the French Quarter, or the rest of the city for that matter. After all, the HRC is just a burger joint with guitars on the wall. The burgers aren't even very good.

Isaac returned with Dan Aykroyd and the Aerosmith boys in tow and redeemed himself to some degree when he opened the House of Blues. The food is mediocre, the hats and T-shirts are overpriced, but the music is good and there's lots of it. Big names, local talent, and even the obscure legends appear on a regular basis. Don't get cocky, Isaac; you're still an outsider.

Margaritaville 1104 Decatur St. (592-2565) Unlike the aforementioned Mr. Tigrett, Jimmy Buffett has some New Orleans roots and occasionally shows up with his Coral Reefers at the Decatur Street branch of the club named after his most commercially successful single. The tropical mystique Buffett created in Key West translated and transplanted well to the French Quarter. The music is mostly of the homegrown variety but stylistically covers the spectrum. The club is large and comfortable with table seating. Don't get cocky, Jimmy; we still think you looked better with a mustache.

Cafe Brasil Frenchmen at Chartres (947-9386) If you want to get down, get gritty, and experience good, clean, animalistic hedonism, troop on over to the Marigny to Cafe Brasil. The joint started out as a coffeehouse and ended up as a dance hall. There are so few places to sit in this cavernous room, you may as well dance and sweat. The music is occasionally of the Latin-American variety but could just as easily be R&B, reggae, folk, rock, Klezmer, Ska, or whatever else one could put a label on.

The Howlin' Wolf 828 S. Peters (523-2551) You can bet that on any given night they're probably howling over at the Howlin' Wolf, located in an old warehouse and, guess where, . . . the Warehouse District. The Wolf has atmosphere and good music with the likes of the subdudes and the Continental Drifters. Sundays in the summer is country music and free barbecue. Monday is open-mike night, when the best songwriters in town stop by to play solo and often jam with their musical brethren.

The Mermaid Lounge 1100 Constance (524-4747) A group of local musicians bought this small, funky wharf bar hidden away downtown as a casual gathering place for friends. Now it's one of the hippest alternative music spots in town. Call for directions, and be ready for a very unusual experience.

Checkpoint Charlie's 501 Esplanade (947-0979) Music and the most eclectic clientele in the city: old hippies, young skateboarding punks, and everything in between. The musical variety is almost as broad. Never no cover.

THE DANCE CLUBS

The Crystal 1135 Decatur St. (586-0339) Has been through many incarnations over the years and currently exists as a dance club where everyone wears black and has spiked hair. This is the place where the bouncer knocked out a millionaire baseball pitcher and Pearl Jam's Eddie Vedder was arrested for being drunk and disorderly (all on the same night). Can you imagine what it takes to get arrested for drunkenness in New Orleans?

City Lights 1000 S. Peters (568-1700) The Warehouse District's terribly chic, trendy, and pretentious night spot. Groovy dudes and foxy chicks stand in long lines and pay a high cover charge for the opportunity to mingle, dance, rap, and see who can be the most aloof.

The Lakefront There are several clubs out at West End that feature recorded dance music, with occasional live music.

LOCAL CHARACTERS

New Orleans loves and nurtures its eccentrics. These are some of the more colorful and well known figures:

Ruthie the Duck Lady was voted as New Orleans' most popular character by the readers of Gambit, *a local weekly. She can often be seen outside Pat O'Brien's with her duck peeping from his cardboard box.*

The Button Lady is also known as the Magic Bean Lady. She fancies platinum wigs and has recently taken to industrial accessories such as a stainless-steel hard hat and hose-clamp bracelets.

The Swami used to drape himself in black sheets and try to sell pamphlets espousing the virtues of some presumably Eastern religion. Lately he can be found at the corner of Baronne and Common streets, where, bearded and barefoot, he bids good morning to the downtown office workers as they head for another day at the high rise.

When you're exploring the French Quarter you may run across a rotund gentleman sporting a bushy red beard and likely wearing a caftan, muumuu, or in sixties fashion parlance, a dashiki. Introduce yourself to Mike Stark. In the era of all things hip, Mike was known as Reverend Mike Stark. He was the activist for the Quarter's hip community and a vital part of the free clinic, known as the H.E.A.D. Clinic. (As an aside, the full name was the Health and Emergency Aid Dispensary, but H.E.A.D. was an appropriate name for as many reasons as your most bizarre flight of fantasy might fathom.) The Reverend Mike Stark was always at the forefront of any campaign of the conscience. In a later incarnation, he was the director of the Flea Market.

In recent years, Mike has made his mark on the planet as a creator of some of the finest Mardi Gras masks to be found anywhere. These ornate leather and feather creations are truly works of art. Check them out at his Little Shop of Fantasy in the 500 block of Dumaine Street.

Drinking
Establishments

The international reputation of New Orleans is that of a "party town." When all the connotations of this label are considered, the single most conspicuous element is the consumption of alcoholic beverages. New Orleans is a great drinking town, and the social structure of the city revolves around the bars. Everyone has a favorite bistro where they go to relax, drink, and visit with friends. There are more bars per capita in New Orleans than any other city in the world.

The New Orleans bar *extraordinaire* is **Pat O'Brien's**. This is not a tourist trap. Many people go here—tourists and locals alike. The drinks are excellent and the prices very reasonable. Pat O'Brien's is a complex of two lounge areas and a beautiful courtyard. The main bar, offering inexpensive drinks, is the first door to the left—a great place to mix and mingle. The lounge to the right is the piano bar. The entertainment is first rate and a good time is assured. There is no cover charge here,

---

MYTH OF THE MINT JULEP

If you are expecting a Gone with the Wind *scenario and mentality in New Orleans, then you will be very surprised! New Orleans is unlike the rest of Louisiana and quite different from the remainder of the South. Ours is a cosmopolitan city comprised of an extremely diverse heritage. There is no typical native New Orleanian. Accents vary throughout the city and defy classification. This is a port city, and Colonel Sanders does not live here, nor does Scarlett O'Hara.*

---

but you must wait to be seated. The patio is scarcely to be believed. An afternoon or evening spent sipping cocktails on the patio at Pat O'Brien's is one of life's truly wonderful experiences. The sights, sounds, and sensations are certain to please.

Pat O'Brien's is world renowned for exotic drinks, primarily the Hurricane. There is an extensive list of house specialties. Most are pleasant and *potent!*

Nick's Across the street from the Dixie brewery in the 2400 block of Tulane Avenue. The local rites of passage to adulthood always include a few visits to Nick's. The building is less than spectacular and borders on being shabby, but inside you will find patrons from all walks of life and every drink imaginable. Nick's reputation was built on his ability to mix any drink named by anyone.

Cosimo's 1201 Burgundy A fine French Quarter neighborhood bar, this is a great place to sit, drink, and talk. Cosimo's is usually low key, but on occasion has been rumored to be the scene of some pretty frenzied dancing.

Johnny White's 733 St. Peter Across the street from Pat O'Brien's, Johnny White's caters mainly to a crowd of Quarterites.

Port of Call 838 Esplanade Besides an excellent kitchen (see **Food**), Port of Call has a bar with its own following. The regular bar fare is offered, as well as some exotic tropical drinks for the more adventurous.

Molly's at the Market 1107 Decatur The irrepressible Jim Monaghan holds court in this Decatur Street wateringhole. Monaghan is an outspoken French Quarter activist and sells probably the best Irish coffee in town.

BEST SELECTION OF BOTTLED IMPORTS:
Cooter Brown's (Carrollton at St. Charles)

F&M Patio 4841 Tchoupitoulas St. A favorite late-night place to go where the crowd gets crazy is the F&M Patio on Tchoupitoulas Street. This was a legendary hangout in the early sixties that returned to life in the late seventies and continues to thrive. The crowd is usually the hard cores coming from Tip's or others who have done the town and just can't go home yet. Great jukebox.

Lafitte's Blacksmith Shop The historic but inconspicuous building at 904 Bourbon is actually one of the quietest and most delightful drinking establishments in town. A fabulous place for a romantic rendezvous—jus' ax Jean!

Fat Harry's 4330 St. Charles Featuring Loyola students and alumni and a good jukebox, Harry's provides a place to eat until about 6 A.M.

Le Bon Temps Roule 4801 Magazine Hard to go wrong at a bar called "The Good Times Roll." Eclectic crowd and interesting atmosphere.

Bruno's, **Boot**, and **Audubon Tavern** are all located near the universities and cater to university students.

Every neighborhood has its own bars; obviously, they are too numerous to mention. Ask anyone who is familiar with a particular neighborhood and you are certain to find one or more to your liking.

Happy Hour

The most renowned happy hour in town is found on Wednesday afternoons at **Jason's** (formerly Que Sera). Young professionals, med techs from the nearby medical centers, college students, you name it, show up for the three-for-one cocktails, but more importantly, to be seen. The crowd spills out of

---

BEST SELECTION OF DRAFTS:
Bulldog on Magazine and Cooter Brown's

the bar and patio onto St. Charles Avenue. If you have your heart set on meeting an inhalation therapist, this is the place for you. 3636 St. Charles Ave.

Also try **Charley G's**, **the Beach Corner, Parlay's, Liuzza's, Robear's, Vic's Kangaroo Cafe,** and **Ernst Cafe**.

BEST SPORTS BAR: Parkway Tavern, 5135 Canal Blvd.

Civilized Pleasures

Sometimes even the wildest party animal wants to sit down, have a drink, and talk to friends without the distractions of lounge lizards on the prowl or thousands of decibels of rock music assaulting the eardrums. When that desire becomes so overwhelming it can no longer be resisted, there are three places to soothe the psyche and engage in the disappearing art of conversation.

The Napoleon House

This New Orleans landmark was formerly the home of Mayor Nicholas Girod, who plotted to rescue the exiled emperor and spirit him to this French Quarter refuge. Napoleon died before his Louisiana saviors could hatch their plot, but the Napoleon House is still a haven where one can escape the pressures and demands of the outside world. Classical music is played in the background, and the crowd ranges from Bohemians to businessmen. There is a pleasant patio, and when the weather permits, the French doors of the main room are opened to create a sidewalk-café-type atmosphere. The food is also very good if the hungries intrude.

The Columns Hotel

The Columns is a National Historic Landmark located among the oaks on St. Charles Avenue. The hotel has traditional rooms for overnight guests and a somewhat fancy restaurant. The primary attraction, though, is the Victorian Bar. A few years back, *Esquire* magazine named the Columns as one of the best bars in the country, and that was before there was seating available on the massive front porch. An afternoon or evening spent on the veranda at the Columns is one of those events in life to be savored. When all the elements are right, you can relive those beer commercials and truly mean it when you say, "Folks, it just doesn't get any better than this!"

Cafe Degas

We are adding a third "civilized pleasure" for the first time. This is the Parisian café of New Orleans. Located in the Faubourg St. John, it faces Esplanade so you can enjoy the avenue and the café's ambience over French bread, wine, and cheese. *Très romantique.*

YE OLDE PIPE SHOPPE

The use of tobacco products—in all forms—has proven to be so hazardous to living things that we hate to endorse anything even remotely affiliated with the evil substance. But . . . both of you individuals out there who still partake, and even the other 99.99 percent of the population who don't, will want to stop by Ye Olde Pipe Shoppe (306 Chartres, established 1868) and visit with the proprietor, Edwin Jansen. Mr. Jansen is the third generation to dispense pipes, tobacco, and wisdom from the shop, which was opened by his grandfather shortly after the Civil War—the military conflict, not the television miniseries.

In his younger days, Mr. Jansen also used to fix watches at a bench behind the display cases. These days he sells pipes, including his own brand of briarwood, and his special blend of tobacco. These blends are stored in gallon jars that rest on shelves attached to the back wall. The sign above reads, Jansen's Tobacco Bar.

There is also an extensive collection of antique pipes. Taking a bit of poetic license, we could refer to the shop as a pipe museum.

Besides pipes and associated pipe paraphernalia, cigars are available if that is your particular vice. Even a tobacconist has to draw the line somewhere, and this one will not sell cigarettes.

Mardi Gras

Imagine over one million revelers in the streets of New Orleans in a euphoric, oblivious, carefree state of mind on Fat Tuesday before Ash Wednesday—painted faces, nudity, marching jazz clubs, black Indians, endless parades, a warm sea of humanity, and the bizarre. A drug trip, you say? No, just the state of mind known as Mardi Gras—the final word on celebration in one giant party where the entire world is invited.

It is billed as the "greatest free show on Earth," but the only things that are free are the sights and the sounds. Prices, especially in the French Quarter, are inflated for the Mardi Gras season, which begins on January 6. But the sights and sounds are priceless, especially on Mardi Gras Day, Fat Tuesday—the last feast day before the fasting of Lent begins.

Various Krewes, or carnival clubs, sponsor dozens of parades during the season, as well as Mardi Gras balls. Enjoy the parades, because you're not invited to the balls (neither are we!). They are strictly private and are a traditional stronghold of elite, upper-class society. But as peasants we can really enjoy the street carnival! Catch a doubloon from a passing float, or see the Zulu Parade on Mardi Gras Day, where you may be fortunate enough to snare a coconut. Try to catch the Mardi Gras Indians and roving jazz clubs as well.

The French Quarter on Mardi Gras Day

For the most party-minded, the French Quarter is the heart of the city on Mardi Gras Day. The atmosphere is pulsating. Arise early and watch the costume party at the corner of Bourbon and Dumaine. This is the beginning of your unforgettable day.

Be a true native and wear a costume or mask for Mardi Gras—you'll enjoy it more. Incidentally, the colors of the carnival season are purple, green, and gold, just in case you're curious about that common combination.

Have fun until midnight, because traditionally all of the streets are cleared at that time by police and you must then use the sidewalks only. As if by magic, officialdom makes Mardi Gras disappear. Poof! The street cleaners then begin the laborious task of clearing more garbage off the streets of New Orleans in one day than Chicago has in a month.

Outside the French Quarter

Up the parade route on St. Charles is where the families gather. The curbs on either side of the avenue are wall-to-wall ladders and platforms of every description. Some go up the

---

BEST TOURIST ADVICE:
Don't wear jewelry to Mardi Gras parades

night before but this practice is technically illegal. The majority are placed in the predawn hours of carnival day.

The promenade starts by 7 A.M. with families and groups costumed alike or with similar themes. Both sanctioned and outlaw marching clubs pass down the street every few minutes. You may encounter Pete Fountain and his Half Fast Marching Club, the Jefferson City Buzzards, or a gang of Tulane students wearing diapers and pushing a stereo system in a shopping cart.

After the Rex Parade passes, the Krewes of Elks and Orleanians roll. These parades consist of miles of trucks, each pulling a float (created by individual clubs). No bands, no horses, just floats. The kids can fill their bags with so much loot you'll have to rent a truck to take it all home.

Parades

Everyone has their favorite parades, and we are no exception. The early parade that we rate highly is **Carrollton**. The weekend prior to Fat Tuesday is the parade time for the so-called Superkrewes, **Endymion** on Saturday and **Bacchus** on Sunday. These are newer Krewes founded in the late sixties by the city's nouveau riche.

In 1994, the famous New Orleans export, Harry Connick, Jr., founded his own Krewe, Orpheus. He brought several of his famous friends to ride with him. This parade is of the Superkrewe variety and parades uptown the Monday night

---

KING CAKE PARTIES

Soon after New Year's and up until Mardi Gras Day, the traditional King cake parties are held in celebration of Mardi Gras. King cakes are sold in January and February at all New Orleans bakeries. Each cake contains a miniature baby doll. The guest whose slice of cake contains this object is expected to throw the next party. King cakes have become big business and are shipped worldwide.

before Fat Tuesday. On carnival day get out early to see **Zulu** and then see the king of carnival in the **Rex** Parade.

The Renegades

If the Krewes who sponsor the major parades are the cream of New Orleans society, these renegades are the soul. These "other" Krewes are much more accessible than those groups who mount the lavish public spectacles that the world has come to know as Mardi Gras. One such alternative group is the **Mystic Orphans and Misfits**. The MOMS ball is held the Saturday night before carnival day and is the legendary wild party. Ask around for the particulars.

Mardi Gras Music

Virtually everyone who can play three chords on a guitar and who has been to carnival has written a song about Mardi Gras. Very few have become classics. Even Paul Simon's "Take Me to the Mardi Gras" hasn't achieved this exalted status. The definitive Mardi Gras numbers are "Mardi Gras Mambo," by a teenaged Art Neville and the Hawkettes, "Carnival Time" by Al Johnson, "Second Line Parts I and II" by Stop Inc., and Professor Longhair's "Go to the Mardi Gras." All these tunes can be found on a compilation album with the original title *Mardi Gras in New Orleans*. The liner notes include a history of each song.

Mardi Gras Indians

The Mardi Gras Indian tribes are groups of black New Orleanians who are carrying on a singing, dancing, marching, music-playing tradition that has been around for more than a hundred years. One of the Indian songs proudly proclaims that "every year at carnival time, we make a new suit." It's not quite true—these groups work all year to create their ornate costumes, which are splendid combinations of plumage and intricate beadwork. The costumes are worn for the year's three parade days. The first Indian parades are obviously on Mardi Gras Day. The second parade day, oddly, is an Italian holiday, St.

Joseph's day, March 19. The third, known as "Super Sunday," takes place during the Jazz Festival.

The tradition originated in African and Caribbean cultures. In the early days in New Orleans, the tribes were basically gangs that tried to outdo each other's costumes and paraded on their own turf. Quite often their paths crossed and blood was shed. Today, the tribal relations are more cordial.

As the Indians march, they play percussion instruments and sing chants. An example of an Indian chant is "Iko Iko," which has been recorded by the Dixie Cups, Dr. John, and others, and was featured in the film *Rain Man*. The opening line, "My spy boy told your spy boy . . ." refers to the tribe's spy boy, an advance man who checks out the territory ahead of the Big Chief and the rest of the tribe.

There are now about a dozen tribes in existence, with names like the Wild Magnolias, the Wild Tchoupitoulas, the Golden Eagles, and the Guardians of the Flame. Their turf is located in and around the New Orleans housing projects. Pick up Dr. John's Grammy-winning CD, *Going Back to New Orleans*, and learn more about the tribes from his song "My Indian Red."

LUNDI GRAS

Quickly becoming a new tradition, Lundi Gras (the Monday before Mardi Gras) may grow so big as an all-day and -night celebration that it could merge with Mardi Gras to make a full-blown Monday-Tuesday event. Try Woldenberg Park, Spanish Plaza, or rent a balcony spot at Patout's on Bourbon.

Jazz Fest

The New Orleans Jazz and Heritage Festival is an event of local, national, and international importance. This celebration of music and culture is held each spring in late April through early May. The Jazz Fest is many things to many people. To some it is a culinary delight, providing an opportunity to sample many local delicacies. To others it is an exhibition by some of the region's and the nation's outstanding craftsmen. The musical portion of the festival is one of America's premier musical celebrations, featuring jazz, blues, gospel, Cajun, zydeco, country and western, and if there's anything we've forgotten, it's there, too! In addition, the heritage fair is a wonderful social outing, and an opportunity to meet old friends and make new ones.

The Jazz Fest consists of a series of nighttime concerts that cover a period of about two weeks. These concerts take place in a variety of concert halls around the city and feature the super-stars of the music industry, such as Ella Fitzgerald, Fats Domino, Wynton Marsalis, and on ad infinitum. Many of these musical giants are also scheduled for appearances at the fairgrounds.

JAZZ FEST POSTERS

In the mid-seventies, a Tulane University student took a course in entrepreneurship. His idea was to produce silk-screen posters suitable for framing. The New Orleans Jazz Festival was just beginning to blossom, so he commissioned Stephanie Dinkins, a local artist, to do the artwork commemorating the event. This was the birth of Pro Creations and a new tradition of the Jazz Fest Poster. The first poster sold then for five dollars and now sells for over a thousand. The current posters come in signed and unsigned editions and always sell out during Jazz Fest. They are available at the Fair Grounds and galleries all over town.

During the two-week period of Jazz Fest, there are so many musicians in town that the music clubs are overflowing with talent. Many of the groups in town for the Fest are booked into clubs. Other musicians show up for the performances and can't resist an invitation to sit in. The result is usually an extended jam session of the world's superlative musicians that only occurs once in a lifetime.

The daytime heritage fair begins around 11 A.M. and ends around 7 P.M. on each of two successive weekends. The food booths are sponsored by some of New Orleans' preeminent restaurateurs, as well as by independent vendors. One should

The Gospel Tent

try to sample a variety of dishes from these booths.

The food booths at the fair used to dispense po' boys, jambalaya, gumbo, and a few other indigenous dishes. You can still sample all of the above and much, much more. Many booths serve combination plates of such exotic items as oyster and tasso pasta, crawfish salad, or spinach and artichoke casserole. The crawfish sack, a variation of a crawfish pie, has received the best word of mouth at recent festivals. The ethnic foods in Congo Square are also worth your sampling.

The craftsmen at the fair are selected through a rigorous screening process to ensure top-quality items. The wares on display run the gamut from the traditional handmade quilts and musical instruments to the more contemporary stained glass and pottery. There are also demonstrations by craftsmen of such traditional skills as chair caning, blacksmithing, and Cajun accordion making.

The musical portion of the fair takes place on several stages and in gazebos and tents located around the fairgrounds. The variety of music is mind boggling; it is virtually impossible to see and hear everything. The acts range from the obscure to the nationally prominent. The best strategy is to get a schedule and devise a plan of movement for the day according to the locations of performances one wishes to attend. As you move from stage to stage, you can take in the crafts and often participate in an impromptu parade.

Survival at the Fair

In order to enjoy the fair to the fullest, there are some things you need to know. Dress comfortably. At this time of the year, the weather has not yet reached its peak of heat and humidity but it can still get pretty warm. A rugged pair of shorts and a T-shirt are recommended, as are comfortable shoes and a hat. If rain is falling, or has fallen in the past 24 hours, expect to get muddy. If it's not raining, pack the sunscreen. Women may also want to take some toilet paper if nature calls. Banks of portable toilets stand at the ready, and Jazz Fest is the testing ground for the futuristic prototypes.

The fair has been expanded to seven days. The first weekend is Friday, Saturday, and Sunday. The second weekend begins on Thursday. In the old days, the first Friday was the day the locals shirked responsibility to kick off the Fest. It was a big local party where you could meet up with old friends you only see once or twice a year. As the popularity grew, the reunions were haphazard and brief in the midst of several thousand people. Locals lamented the lost tradition and the Thursday date of the second week was added as an accommodation.

This all leads to the point that the crowds have become huge and have a tendency to build as the weekend progresses. Sunday afternoon around 4 (both weekends) is when the crowds peak. If you suspect you may be claustrophobic, this is not the time to put those suspicions to the test.

Getting to the fairgrounds is best accomplished by shuttle bus, RTA bus, cab, or any other means that doesn't require the burden of driving in traffic and attempting to park where there are no places. Early birds can pay to park inside the fairgrounds. If you do, you can keep supplies in your car and restock as necessary. If you park in the surrounding neighborhoods, keep a reasonable distance from driveways, fire hydrants, and corners. The meter maids have measuring tapes and 15 feet is the rule. Additionally, all the city's tow trucks will be concentrated in the area and form a constant parade to the auto pound.

Our final words to the wise: take lots of money and/or credit cards. There is so much to buy—food, beer, music, crafts, T-shirts, posters, and every other thing you can imagine. In recent years, an automatic teller has been added for those who have limited self-control or unlimited resources.

Other Fairs and Festivals

There are hundreds of fairs and festivals within driving range. Here is a local sampling.

The French Quarter Festival

This was conceived as an effort to lure the locals back to the Quarter. It succeeded. There are stages set up to showcase New Orleans musicians on nearly every corner. Riverboat racing on the Mississippi and historical lectures and tours are some of the highlights of this early-spring event.

Festa d'Italia

The city's Italian heritage is the focus of this festival, held every October at the obvious location of the Piazza d'Italia on Poydras Street. There are always some spicy meatballs and many other Italian edibles to munch on while you watch the bocce-ball tournament.

NEW ORLEANS BEER FESTIVAL

The beginning of our sweltering summers becomes much more bearable with the annual Beer Festival. The New Orleans Fair Grounds is the site of this WYES-TV public television fund raiser. The modest price of admission covers all of the beer you care to savor, plus a nice array of food catered by local restaurants and delis. This is a delightful afternoon for the adult beer connoisseur, with offerings of over a hundred different imported, home-brewed, and microbrewery beers. We recommend a designated driver or a taxi home. WYES-TV does a much more sophisticated Wine Festival in the fall.

Jeff Fest

When autumn comes rolling around, the best musical festival in the metro area is held at Lafreniere Park. Yeah, you rite! We even rock in the suburbs. The party is called the Jeff Fest and is held in October. This is what the Jazz Fest was in 1970. A few big-name headliners like Leon Russell and Marcia Ball draw the crowds and the best of the local groups keep the two-day party swinging. One daily admission (which has been most reasonable in the past) allows access to all the music. Food booths offer sustenance, the grounds are spacious, and the crowds are not overwhelming. Oops, we've done it again. Another secret is revealed and another great event will be overrun with humanity. What the heck, let's dance.

The Cutting Edge

Just when you thought life couldn't get any better, along came the Cutting Edge Music Conference. Another early-fall event, the Cutting Edge was conceived to facilitate the business of music, similar to Austin's South by Southwest affair.

Record-company executives are in attendance to survey the talent. Other entertainment professionals offer seminars and workshops to assist musicians in their business transactions.

Then, there is the music. Bands, groups, ensembles, and individuals of every musical genre pack the city for the three-day conference. The clubs showcase the talent in multi-act line-ups. You can pay one price and ride shuttle buses between the various venues. Stay out late and take it all in.

Tomato Festival

The Louisiana Creole tomato is celebrated at the French Market's Tomato Festival in June. The festival heralds the arrival of our indigenous strain of this vegetable (or is it a fruit?) to the Market.

Mirliton Festival

This is Bywater's contribution to the festival craze. Is it pronounced "mella-tahn" or "merla-tahn"? No one seems to care because the various foods cooked at the festival are sensational. And if you can't pronounce it, just call it an alligator pear.

The Louisiana Swamp Festival

This is held at the Audubon Zoo in the fall and pays homage to the Cajun way of life. Plenty of good food and music over two weekends. Normal zoo admission fee.

St. Patrick's Day

There are at least three officially sanctioned parades and who knows how many outlaw bands of roving Irishmen taking to the streets to honor St. Patrick. The Irish Channel parade is usually the Saturday afternoon before St. Paddy's, and the crowd congregates early at Parasol's in the Irish Channel. The Metairie parade takes place on the Sunday afternoon prior to the big day, and is centered around Pat Gillen's on Metairie Road. The French Quarter parade is at night, and the place to be is Jim Monaghan's Molly's at the Market on Decatur Street. The green cabbages fly from the floats and the green beer gushes from the taps. If St. Paddy's Day doesn't happen to fall on a weekend, then when March 17 actually arrives, the aforementioned taverns once again overflow with normally respectable, conservative Irishmen sporting green faces and leprechaun ears.

St. Joseph's Day

Another Catholic celebration, this one Italian. The tradition is that families set up altars to St. Joseph consisting of massive food displays. These private homes are then open to the public for viewing and sometimes sampling before the altars are dismantled and the food given to the needy.

Greek Festival

Held in May of each year at the Hellenic Center on Robert E. Lee at Bayou St. John. Try some baklava while you watch the Spyridons and Psarellis demonstrate Greek folk dances.

Half-Shell Award: The Tennessee Williams/ New Orleans Literary Festival

This has grown in just a very short time into an orgy (Tennessee would have liked the choice of word) of plays, readings, performances, and literary tours. The activity is centered around Le Petit Theatre at the corner of St. Peter and Chartres on Jackson Square. Le Petit produces one of the Williams plays and is the scene of many of the other events.

Besides celebrating Tennessee, the literary festival also pays tribute to other Louisiana writers and Southern writers in general, both past and present. Some of the local novelists who have been participants and/or topics of discussion include Anne Rice, creator of the seductive Vampire Lestat, and mystery writer Tony Fennelly. Early spring.

The New Orleans Film and Video Festival

This is held each fall as a showcase for local producers and directors, and premieres new films from the major studios. The program is still young (its maiden voyage was in 1989), but came of age in 1993 under the guidance of programmer John Desplas. In '93, the program featured pre-release viewing of the latest by legendary Robert Altman and emerging talent Gus Van Sant. Look out, Sundance!

There are many annual festivals, and many others that are held on a one-time basis. Someone celebrates something on most any weekend. Check the entertainment listings in the Friday *Times-Picayune* Lagniappe section for current information.

New Orleans Medley

Barber Stories

Besides consulting our book, if you want the scoop on what's happening in New Orleans there are two very "reliable" sources: bartenders and barbers. For three generations the Grahams have been getting haircuts from Sal's International, now located at 1536 Robert E. Lee. This is not uncommon at Sal's, where some natives have been clipped and sheared for four generations. The original 1963 crew of barbers remains loyal at Sal's.

According to Judy Pesses, employee *extraordinaire*, "This group at Sal's is truly the last of a breed. People aren't aware that barbers are extinct." Whether it's Armand, Randy, Ronnie, Les, Lloyd, Leo, or Sal himself, these barbers and others can tell some great stories about New Orleans and the heads of hair they've cut, as a random sampling will show. Did you hear what happened when:

New Orleans' own Pulitzer Prize winner for military history nearly duked it out with the man in the next chair concerning the writer's facts v. the ex-D-Day participants' story?

An absentminded professor took the wrong coat (never mind that it was several sizes off) after his haircut and the barbers tracked him down by calling the university operator and describing the professor whose name they did not know? (And we think we have reputations!)

A snake got loose in the barbershop?

The prominent former Jesuit High School head football coach threw up everywhere?

Randy was pushing venison sausage on the side (was it really venison)?

Sal evacuated the shop due to a bomb scare after a man's hair was cut too short? And then one customer insisted that his haircut be finished, and the barber actually complied?

Sal was featured by the local author Mary Lou Widmer in *New Orleans in the Fifties*?

The power went out and the barbers went outside to cut hair using the veterinarian's electricity?

Al Hirt, Wayne Mack, Mel Leavitt, Henry Dupree, and Pete Fountain were all regulars (Pete, with hair?)?

The local ventriloquist, while in the chair, turned the shop into chaos?

There are hundreds of amusing stories like these that make up our New Orleans cultural and social "history." You want more? Go by Sal's, especially around holidays for the open bar, refreshments, and decorations. You'll get an earful from any of the barbers and you can bet each Barber Story is 100 percent accurate.

Bells Will Be Ringing

There are pros and cons to living in a Catholic city. But the joy of residing in Catholic New Orleans is a great counterforce to the exaggerated Protestant work ethic evidenced by the daily jams on I-10. Wherever you go or live in New Orleans, even in the suburbs, you are never far from a Catholic church. What this means is that you hear bells chiming beautifully at pleasant intervals. This is a cultural advantage, if you pause and listen.

The effect, even to us heathens, is almost centering. The bells provide a needed respite from our complex, regimented world. They transform us from harried beings into serene ones. The calming pause might be brief but it can sustain us for hours.

A favorite and unforgettable stroll or run is along Bayou St. John near Pitot House. When the bells from Our Lady of the Rosary chime at sunset as you walk across the pedestrian bridge, you become magically transported to another, simpler place and time—the Old World. The historic link to France and Spain is the foundation of New Orleans and gives us this daily musical reminder.

Catholicism defines so much of what we do here. True, it is a very distorted definition but we must credit the "Catlicks" for our wonderfully maverick reality. Almost everyone possesses a let-your-hair-down mentality. After all, who wants to be dead and buried knowing they've never properly embarrassed themselves, their friends, and their family—at least once?

VOODOO (WHO DO?)

If you do, then you know the voodoo queen of New Orleans, Marie Laveau, has been celebrated in songs, books, television, and every other medium you can imagine. Marie has allegedly been buried over in the St. Louis No. 1 cemetery for quite some time. We know for certain there is a tomb bearing her name but there are rumors that Marie lives on. If she is not here in body, she most definitely is present in spirit.

We have heard there are many among us who dabble in the art of voodoo and others who practice religiously. There is ample evidence in the cemeteries after sacred-day rituals.

If the supernatural occasionally invades your realm of consciousness, you'll be pleased to learn that there are several establishments where one can actively channel or summon the spirits. The practitioner can also purchase those necessary ingredients, potions, and hardware essential to the well-stocked medicine chest of the nineties.

If you want your readings done, whether it be tea leaves, tarot cards, or the old reliable crystal ball, visit **The Bottom of the Cup Tearoom.** *This place has been around since the thirties and it would seem that, in this particular line of work, its longevity is a testament to its quality. Those who commune with the spirits are usually a nomadic tribe, whether by choice or necessity.*

Catholic confessions and palm reading are apparently best

performed in privacy, and the BOTC aims to please with a wall full of curtained confessionals. If you're a bit squeamish or lack total conviction, the shop on Conti Street is spacious, clean, and well lit. The branch office on Royal is more cluttered and doesn't seem quite as safe.

If safety is your concern, you'll want to avoid the darker elements at the **Voodoo Museum** *on Dumaine Street. This is where one can purchase the more sordid elements of the art such as various parts of cold-blooded creatures. These items are sold in the gift shop. Take some home for the nephew's graduation present. The museum staff will even instruct you in the proper utilization.*

You exhibitionists in the audience, those who prefer to do it in public, can have your cards read and your fortune told by one of the many soothsayers around Jackson Square. In recent years, they have multiplied faster than pigeons. Like the pigeons, if you don't feed them, they might go away.

The Bottom of the Cup *616 Conti (524-1997), and 732 Royal (523-1204)*

Voodoo Museum *724 Dumaine (523-7685)*

Political Realities

"What, me worry?" This lighthearted quote is attributed to Alfred E. Newman, but the adage can be aptly applied to the political attitude adjustment of metro natives. Certainly bouts of seriousness in the history of New Orleans politics exist. However, these occasions are short-lived. Frivolity always emerges in festive fashion either to halt reform or cause us to forget the question.

No sooner do things become politically heated at the grassroots level, than along comes another of the renowned New Orleans 200-plus festivals, celebrations, or merrymaking enjoyments. These occasions of course include the "Big Three" diversions (Mardi Gras, Jazz Fest, and the Saints) that preoccupy us nearly eight months of the year. Stir this in with sweltering summers (when seriousness is a newcomer's faux pas) and we're left with, say, three weeks a year to be outspokenly serious. The regretful results of our accepting, carefree attitude are: open drainage canals, potholes, the polluted Dead Sea called Pontchartrain, segregated dual school systems, Veterans Highway blight, and grossly disparate socioeconomic classes—basically, the ills of urban America.

New Orleanians are not all apathetic. We do, however, prioritize, and revelry is our raison d'etre. It is our heritage. A Civil War example best illustrates our perverse political leanings, which are neither left nor right, but remarkably slanted nonetheless.

New Orleans was considered a strategic target for the Union's plan to control the Mississippi River and cut the South in half. Following a ferocious exchange of firepower downriver near the Gulf of Mexico, Admiral Farragut's fleet steamed past the gallant Confederate forts on either side of the Mississippi. All that lay between the Yankee navy and the city were surface-breaking alligator garfish.

The Rebel army furiously began to fortify for the invasion. The "Second Battle of New Orleans" promised to be hard fought and would most assuredly take its historic place with Vicksburg in the annals of Civil War history. But the battle never happened.

Bombs bursting in air? Levees destroyed and the city flooded? Fires in the French Quarter? Blood spilled on the corner of First Street and Chestnut in the Garden District? This was unfathomable to the city fathers. Was a battle really necessary? Let's be reasonable. After all, the South wasn't faring very well at this point in the war. Basin Street bookies were giving the North odds at 50 to 1. In perhaps the most unheralded act of preservation during the entire Civil War, our city's pragmatic politicians convinced the dismayed Confederate commander to surrender before a shot was fired. The Krewe of Rex could still roll. What, me worry?

WHERE'S THE BEACH?

Many people come to New Orleans thinking that we're on the Gulf of Mexico. In actuality, New Orleans is about 50 miles north and west of the Gulf Coast. The closest thing we have is Lake Pontchartrain. The lake is good for fishing and boating and the shore is good for sunning and cruising, but **don't go in the water.** *This water is polluted in a big way by runoff from city drainage, untreated or undertreated sewerage from communities on the lake's perimeter, and innumerable other hazards.*

The Arts

Half-Shell Award: The Louisiana Philharmonic Orchestra

Like the city itself, the New Orleans Symphony experienced economic hardship during the mid-eighties and even disbanded entirely for a time. This loss sent shock waves throughout the community and had the symphony's board of directors and the citizenry at large scrambling to raise money to restore it. In 1988, it was resurrected for a couple of seasons and failed again. Finally, the musicians took over and the orchestra took its current, successful form.

In an effort to appeal to the broadest audience possible, concerts are scheduled in a variety of venues and formats. The Classical Series is the traditional orchestra under the direction of guest conductors. This series offers over a dozen productions with three performances of each, and often features a guest instrumental or vocal soloist.

The Blue Jean Series is for the more casually inclined music lover and showcases the work of a particular composer over the length of the series. For the fans of Broadway musicals, the Broadway Pops series offers concert versions of popular musicals such as *Camelot* and *Ain't Misbehavin'*. The kids need their dose of culture, too, and to accommodate them there are the Saturday morning Discovery Concerts. Kinder Concerts and Young People's concerts are held on weekdays and are a cultured alternative to the field trip to the fire station. The LPO performs at the Orpheum Theater, 129 University Pl. (525-0340)

We know of those in the suburbs who would risk cultural malnutrition in front of the tube rather than venture into the wilds of the city to attend a concert. Never fear, suburbanites, the LPO will provide you with your minimum yearly requirement of classical music in its performances under the auspices of the Jefferson Performing Arts Society. Speaking of the JPAS, Dennis Assaf is the guiding force behind this organization and nearly single-handedly supplies the cultural lifeline to the suburbs. (834-5727)

The New Orleans Opera

The New Orleans Opera has been in existence since 1943. The season usually consists of three operas in the fall and one in the spring. This is a permanent company that often imports a prominent main singer for its productions.

There are so many other performing groups in New Orleans that it is impossible to list them all. Every ethnic and special-interest group has its dance and musical performers. Some are well organized and perform regularly; others are loose-knit ensembles that surface sporadically. If you're interested in signing on but don't know where to find the group that performs 16th-century folk songs from the Lithuanian Highlands, call the good folks at the Arts Council. Chances are they can put you in touch with those of similar ilk. (523-1465)

Museums

The Louisiana State Museum is actually a complex of three museums: the Cabildo, the Presbytere, and the U.S. Mint. The Cabildo and the Presbytere flank St. Louis Cathedral at Jackson Square. The Cabildo, on the Canal Street side of the Cathedral, had a near disastrous fire in May of 1988 while it was undergoing a massive restoration. Only the expert work of the New Orleans fire department saved the building and its treasures from total ruin. The top floor and roof, including the distinctive rooftop cupola, were damaged but most of the artifacts, including Napoleon's death mask, were saved. The citizens rallied to the cause and fund raisers were in the works immediately. Pat O'Brien's sold its bar in square-inch parcels to raise restoration funds. The museum has been restored and joins its sister museum, the Presbytere, on the Esplanade side of the Cathedral, in housing Louisiana's heritage.

The U.S. Mint (400 Esplanade) is, as might be supposed, a former U.S. mint turned museum and houses permanent exhibits on carnival and jazz. See **Music.** Admission is charged at all of the Louisiana state museums.

New Orleans Museum of Art NOMA, in City Park, is the crown jewel of the area museums. The permanent collections are spectacular, and the rotating exhibits are always of impeccable quality. NOMA has also hosted traveling extravaganzas such as the King Tut exhibit. Admission.

Confederate Museum 929 Camp St. (523-4522) An obscure little gem of a museum located next to Lee Circle. The South's gonna do it again! Admission.

Historic New Orleans Collection 533 Royal (523-4662) This is the principal depository for vintage photographs and archival material documenting the history of New Orleans. Free.

In addition to the many museums in the area, there are also several historic homes open to the public:

Hermann Grima House 820 St. Louis St. (525-5661)

Gallier House 1118-32 Royal (523-6722)

Beauregard-Keyes House 1113 Chartres (523-7257)

1850 House 523 St. Ann

Pitot House 1440 Moss St. on Bayou St. John (482-0312)

All by admission.

The Pitot house

Theater

The local theater scene is alive and flourishing. There are several stages and groups worthy of your attention.

The Contemporary Arts Center (566-0233) Consistent in its choice of productions and its usually inspired casting. Some of the more notable productions have been *'A' My Name Is Alice*, *Greater Tuna*, and a locally conceived musical, *Where the Girls Were*. The CAC produces a seasonal series of plays, and tickets can be purchased for the individual shows or, at a worthwhile savings, for the entire series. Group rates are also available.

Le Petit Theatre du Vieux Carré 616 St. Peter (522-2081) Located at the corner of St. Peter and Chartres, across the street from the Cabildo. For many years, Le Petit was the domain of the blue-haired social set and was renowned for its mundane play selection. Many feel that is still the case. Regardless, this is the city's oldest consistently operating theater. Le Petit produces an excellent series for children and is the primary venue for the Tennessee Williams Festival held each spring.

Theater Marigny 616 Frenchmen St. (944-2653) A tiny but adventurous theater located, as the name implies, in the Marigny section of town, adjacent to the French Quarter.

The Actors' Warehouse 200 Julia St. (524-8441) A group composed of some of New Orleans' leading stage actors. The company was created to produce mostly one-act plays that are directed, performed, and frequently written by the members. The group set up shop in an extra room off the True Brew Too Coffeehouse, located in the Warehouse District, and also produces a series of plays for children.

Southern Repertory Theater is New Orleans' only Equity company. This means that they use union actors and technicians and must pay union wages. This is a summer series that is beginning to overlap late spring and into early fall. The emphasis is on Southern writers and themes. Various locations.

OTHER THEATERS

The Patchwork Players A children's summertime series at Tulane University.

Summer Lyric Theater Tulane's long-running, high-quality series of musicals.

Tulane Center Stage Another summer series, housed in Tulane's Lupin Theater. Usually high quality productions.

The University of New Orleans hosts the **Theater by the Lake** series at the UNO Performing Arts Center.

If you would like to spend an evening at the theater and are not sure about the play, the following list of local talent is worth watching:

Bob Bruce and David Cuthbert Writers of musical satire, usually with a local flavor.

Vernel Bagneris A local impresario who wrote and directed the internationally acclaimed *One Mo' Time*, its sequel *And Further Mo'*, and the stage rendition of *Stagger Lee*.

Director **Carl Walker**, formerly the theater director at the Contemporary Arts Center, is now plying his trade at various other sites around town.

PLAYWRIGHTS

Jan Villarubia Author of an award-winning play set in a Canal Street cemetery, *Odd Fellows' Rest*.

Jackie Bullock Author of *The Queen of the Swine Festival* and *Caviar*.

Nan Parati

Luis Ortiz

ACTORS/ACTRESSES

In no particular order, and barely scratching the surface of hometown talent:

Jan Jensen

Mark McLaughlin

Clare Moncrief
Danny Bowen
Susan Shumate
Francine Segal
M. Audley Keck
Kathleen Turner
Adella Gautier Zu-Bolton (can also be found entertaining children as Adella-Adella the Story Teller)
John O'Neil
David Tringali
Ginger Guma

DIRECTORS

Paul Werner
George Kelly
Ron Gural
John Grimsley

CABARET

Becky Allen, a comedic veteran of the New Orleans boards, teams up with Ricky Graham for a hilarious musical revue called *Hot Stuff.* Graham's character sketches include celebrities such as Bette Davis and local stereotypes like Marie Antoinette Impastato from Marie Antoinette's Palace of Beauty in downtown Arabi. It's racy. It's hilarious.

Writers

New Orleans and its exotic environs have proven to be a perfect stimulus for many noted American writers. Tennessee Williams maintained a home here until his death and the old streetcar named "Desire" that inspired perhaps his greatest work is on display behind the U.S. Mint museum on Esplanade. William Faulkner, F. Scott Fitzgerald, Sherwood Anderson, and William Burroughs all stopped in New Orleans on the road to the great American novel.

Present-day New Orleans is still a haven for writers of both fact and fiction. Until recently, one of the most successful novelists from the area was Walker Percy. He actually lived across the lake in St. Tammany Parish, saying that New Orleans had too many ghosts, causing one to wonder whether these spirits were personal or public. Be that as it may, we recommend his early tales of the fallen Southern aristocracy such as *The Moviegoer, Lancelot, Love in the Ruins,* and *The Last Gentleman.*

Anne Rice has returned to her childhood home and the haunts of her Vampire Lestat. She now writes from her home in the Garden District.

You would probably never know it from his extensive body of work, but award-winning science-fiction novelist George Alec Effinger's imagination is probably running amok in his French Quarter apartment as you read this passage.

Andrei Codrescu is a commentator for National Public Radio who rides the Greyhound between his New Orleans home and his teaching position at LSU in Baton Rouge. Codrescu's book *Raised by Puppets Only to Be Killed by Research* is a collection of his NPR essays drawn from his astute satiric observations of life in America. He can often be found at Cafe Brasil when he's not nurturing fledgling writers in Baton Rouge. Alice Codrescu is a talented artist in her own "paint" and they occasionally collaborate on productions.

If you're interested in New Orleans music, *Up from the Cradle of Jazz* by Jason Berry, Tad Jones, and Jon Foose traces the

---

OSCAR WILDE

Spanish Fort was erected at the mouth of Bayou St. John at Lake Pontchartrain in 1769. Through the years it was used not only for the obvious military purposes, but also as a lakeside resort, opera house, casino, and luxury restaurant. It was here that the Irish poet Oscar Wilde lectured to thousands in the late 1800s. It is now in ruins, begging for historical preservation.

development of, you guessed it, New Orleans jazz. *I Hear You Knockin'*, by Jeff Hannusch, chronicles New Orleans' contributions to rock 'n' roll.

The definitive New Orleans novel is still John Kennedy Toole's *A Confederacy of Dunces.* Toole captures the essence of the average, everyday Yat in his laughing-out-loud, Pulitzer Prize-winning novel. Ignatius J. Riley's mother is without question the quintessential Irish Channel mama. Toole's earlier novel, *The Neon Bible,* was written at age 16 and is an accomplished work also worthy of your attention.

Several other New Orleans authors whose works admirably capture the spirit and flavor of our city and culture are: Sheila Bosworth, Ellen Gilchrist, and Shirley Anne Grau.

Bookstores

New Orleans of course has the major chain bookstores such as Waldenbooks and B. Dalton. There is also Bookstar (located in the Jax Brewery), which is part of a chain and sells books at a discount. There are also many locally owned new and used bookstores worthy of your attention.

Maple Street Book Shop 7523 Maple St. (866-4916) Maybe the city's oldest and definitely one of the best of the locally owned shops.

Maple Street Children's Book Shop 7529 Maple St. (861-2105) Right next door to the parent shop, so to speak.

DeVille Books Jax Brewery, One Shell Square, and Riverwalk. New, out-of-print, and rare books.

Beaucoup Books 5414 Magazine St. (895-2663) Has a children's reading room and a good selection of travel and children's books.

Little Professor 1000 S. Carrollton Ave. (866-7646) A good general selection, plus a well-stocked music and poetry section for the more cultured among you.

Bayou Books 1005 Monroe St., Gretna, on da Wes' bank (368-1171) New, old, used, and rare books, specializing in Louisiana books.

USED BOOKS

Beckham's 228 Decatur St. (522-9875) A sizeable collection of used classical records as well.

Librairie Book Shop 823 Chartres (525-4837)

Old Books 811 Royal (522-4003)

George Herget Books 3109 Magazine (891-5595) The late, great George had extensive collections of books, sheet music, and postcards. George has gone to his great reward but the store remains open. Your reward is the hidden treasure tucked away in those cluttered shelves.

Public Library

The New Orleans Public Library's main branch is located at 219 Loyola Avenue at Tulane Avenue. Additionally, there are 11 branch libraries. The main library contains an extensive Louisiana division, which includes maps, government documents, manuscripts, and just about anything else you could imagine that deals with the history of the state. The libraries also have everything that major libraries should have, such as films and videos, record albums, compact discs, and audio cassettes, and if the walls of the old homestead are a bit bare or boring, you can even check out paintings to enhance the decor. If you can't find it at the public library, the area's many universities are available for research purposes. Tulane, the University of New Orleans, Loyola, Xavier, and others allow the general public access, but not borrowing privileges.

Latter Library

Do you want to see the inside of one of those grand St. Charles Avenue mansions without having to knock on a stranger's door? Get on the streetcar and tell the conductor to let you off at the Latter Library, or more specifically, the

---

BEST GUIDEBOOK:
New Orleans on the Half-Shell, *hands down*

Milton H. Latter Memorial Library, a stately name for a stately mansion. The house was built in 1907 with materials from around the country and the world. The mahogany for the staircase and paneling came from South America and the chandeliers and mirrors from Czechoslovakia. The craftsmanship likely came from the Irish Channel. Take note of the fresco ceilings and the plaster moldings. The front parlor is an elegant sitting room. Across the hall is the early-20th-century office.

The home was purchased in 1948 by Mr. and Mrs. Harry Latter with the specific intent to transform the structure into a public library. After the Latters modified the premises, the building was donated to the city in memory of their son Milton, a casualty of war.

After you've toured, marvelled, and fantasized, you can stroll the grounds, which cover a square block. If you want to utilize the resources, there are two floors of books, including a large children's collection for the tykes.

Local Publications

The one daily newspaper in New Orleans is *The Times-Picayune*. If you want to read a standard local newspaper, buy it. It's not outstanding, but it doesn't have to be—it's the only game in town. However, the Sunday literature section is excellent due to the efforts of books editor Susan Larson. Are you reading this, Susan?

Lagniappe The Friday *T-P* contains the Lagniappe section, which is the weekly entertainment guide. This section is outstanding and is an indispensable reference for current entertainment listings.

Gambit is a free weekly that serves as an alternative news source. *Gambit* frequently ruffles feathers with its political and investigative reporting. Extensive entertainment listings and reviews are a *Gambit* highlight.

Offbeat magazine is a free monthly that focuses on the New Orleans and regional music and arts scenes. The music coverage is extensive and the writers are knowledgeable and literate. Get it at the record stores, clubs, and coffeehouses.

Sidney's newsstand, at 917 Decatur in the Quarter, is an excellent source of reading material. Magazines, paperbacks, out-of-town newspapers, and racing forms are available.

Art Galleries

Back in the very early eighties, a group of art-gallery owners got together and planned a night on which all the galleries held openings of new exhibits. This evening of openings coincided with the Contemporary Arts Center's annual benefit and chichi happening known as Art for Art's Sake. The event heralds the opening of the cultural season and a return from the horse latitudes of the New Orleans summer.

Once a year, the galleries played host to the hordes, serving beer and wine to any and all who passed through their portals. The early-fall event quickly became a ritual for the arts community. People started coming in costume and renting buses and limousines to drive them from gallery to gallery.

Initially, the galleries were mostly centered on Magazine Street, which provided a long runway to the CAC beginning around Nashville Avenue. Magazine Street still houses many galleries, but many are now clustered around Julia Street. This downtown migration has only spread the party over a larger area.

It's a TV news cliché to say that New Orleans loves a party, but these coordinated openings were so successful for the galleries and so much fun for those in attendance, they are now held on a monthly basis. To find out when the next will occur, call a gallery on Julia Street or Magazine Street to ask when a new exhibit will be opening. Then, follow the crowds—you can't miss it.

Highlight: RHINO Gallery, Canal Place

RHINO is a cooperative of sorts that features a host of local artists working in every medium imaginable. The gallery works include textile, art, sculpture, jewelry, and whatever else you may want or need. Of particular interest is the work of Bruce Benefield and Mitchell Gaudet, the glass blowers from Studio

Inferno. Why, you might ask, is this cornucopia of art named after the rhino, the most aesthetically unpleasing beast? Well, you know what they say about beauty, but zoology notwithstanding, this gallery is *Right Here in New Orleans*.

ART GALLERIES—MAGAZINE STREET

Academy Gallery 5256 Magazine
Carol Robinson Gallery 4537 Magazine
Tilden-Foley Gallery 4119 Magazine
Mario Villa Gallery 3908 Magazine

ART GALLERIES—JULIA STREET

Gasperi Gallery 320 Julia
Arthur Roger Gallery 432 Julia
Marguerite Oestreicher 626 Julia (Jeff Jennings of *Half-Shell* fame exhibits here)

ART GALLERIES—FRENCH QUARTER

A Gallery for Fine Photography 313 Royal St. New Orleans' premier photo gallery, featuring local, national, current, and vintage photographs.
Hanson Galleries 229 Royal St. Fine-art consultant Diana Miller will joyfully and expertly guide you through the galleries. Don't forget the upstairs.
Art Attacks 831 St. Peter St.
Hall-Barnett Gallery 320 Exchange Alley
Animation Sensations 301 Chartres

Note: Many other galleries in the French Quarter and other parts of town also participate in the monthly openings. Check the *Gallery* section in the newspaper or just follow the crowds.

Public Art

The largest accessible fine-art collection in the city can be found at the K&B Plaza on St. Charles Avenue at Lee Circle. The Virlane Foundation is our benefactor. The man behind the foundation is drugstore mogul and arts patron Sidney Besthoff. Get off the streetcar and check out the outdoor sculpture. Enter the foyer of the building and view the paintings. It's there for you. Take advantage of it.

We're not sure if it's really art; however, art, like beauty, is in the eye of the beholder. When you're driving out Esplanade towards City Park and approaching the 2300 block, the same block where a marker commemorates a former residence of impressionist Edgar Degas, you will see the home of a local architect and alleged artist who shall remain anonymous to protect his privacy. He has assembled an ever-changing collection of geometrical figures (trapezoids come to mind but we were never math wizards) made of sheet metal. There are also assemblages of concrete blocks that mutate from time to time to take on new appearances. While the neighbors spend their Saturday mornings weeding and edging, this individual, we imagine, spends his leisure rearranging his blocks and, well, geometrical figures. On occasion, a giant paper-mache swordfish hangs from the porch. However you define art, it's worth the drive to view one man's vision.

THE BOURBON STREET HUSTLE

On your first or second stroll down Bourbon Street, one of the local hustlers is going to approach you with an unbelievable proposition: "Hey mistah [usually the mark is a man], I bet you $5 I can tell you where you got dem shoes." If you don't bite on the first attempt, he will get more specific: "I can tell you the place, the day, and the time where you got dose shoes."

There are those naïve few who can't resist a sure thing, and this bet looks like one and quacks like one. After all, how can this total stranger know that this particular pair of shoes was purchased at 2:15 P.M. on Saturday, April 4, at the suburban shopping mall in Waycross, Ga.? You take the bet—you lose. 'Cause "you got dem shoes on Bourbon Street on February 12 at 9:30 at night." Pay up.

The most celebrated folk art in town is on display at the House of Blues. HOB founder Isaac Tigrett has been a folk-art collector for years. He must have a huge collection because he has covered the walls of the local branch of his latest enterprise.

The owner of Doug's Place in the 700 block of Camp Street is also a folk-art collector. Like Isaac, he has used numerous pieces to adorn his restaurant. Incidentally, this is the building that housed the recording studio where Cosimo Matassa produced some of the greatest music ever to come out of New Orleans. Some of the hit records are also displayed and Doug has created a musical walk of fame with brass music notes set in the concrete floor.

The true New Orleans folk-art collection can be found at the Saturn Bar out at 3067 St. Claude Avenue. The work was produced by a regular customer and neighborhood denizen. After you view the art, mingle with the customers. They could be artists, writers, musicians, movie stars, plumbers, or longshoremen. They're all there at one time or another.

Films in New Orleans

The ad in the trades says, "Shoot the other LA," and that's just what many of Hollywood's directors are doing. Instead of making movies in Los Angeles, they're packing up the cast and crew and transporting the whole bunch to New Orleans and the surrounding areas, where the costs are lower and the environs more cinematic. Over the years there have been many films made in New Orleans, but the past decade in particular has seen a continuous influx of production crews.

Of the many movies made here in New Orleans, the definitive New Orleans film has yet to appear. In fact, no one has even gotten the accent right, not Brando in *Streetcar Named Desire*, not the crawfish lady in *King Creole*, and certainly not Dennis Quaid in *The Big Easy*. Speaking of *The Big Easy*, prior to its release that term was only used by the gossip columnist for *The Times-Picayune* and usually embarrassed everyone else in town. Now it has become America's perception of New Orleans.

The following is a completely arbitrary list of memorable New Orleans films, in no particular order and for varied reasons:

Tightrope   Clint Eastwood's modern *film noir* used New Orleans as an effective backdrop for this murder tale.

Pretty Baby   Brooke Shields' controversial debut as a child prostitute marked Louis Malle's story of photographer E. J. Bellocq.

Hard Times   Before his vigilante days, Charles Bronson played a bare-knuckle brawler on the New Orleans waterfront.

Cat People   This hokey tale of voodoo was most notable for Nastassia Kinski's nude romp through the swamp and the post-premiere party, where a local feminist took offense at director Paul Schrader's portrayal of women and presented him with the proverbial pie in the eye.

Streetcar Named Desire   Homage to Tennessee, Stanley, and Blanche.

The Big Easy   Although a commercial success, this film used every local cliché imaginable, created some new ones, and portrayed everyone as a Cajun. It was partially filmed in Bucktown (remember the Cajun dance scene?).

The Pelican Brief   A John Grisham novel-turned-movie filmed at "Twolane" and starring Julia Roberts.

JFK   The president was not the only victim here. See **Assassination Fascination**.

Assassination Fascination

Conspiracy buffs take note. Only one person ever stood trial for the assassination of John F. Kennedy. Many feel that Oliver Stone and Kevin Costner should have been prosecuted for their assassination of Southern accents and good taste in the movie *JFK*. Unfortunately, as is so often the case in Hollywood, they received accolades rather than censure.

Film criticism aside, the Kennedy assassination trial took place right here in New Orleans. Jim Garrison, the district attorney for Orleans Parish, was convinced, as was/is the majority of the rational world, that the Warren Commission was wrong. Garrison's disbelief, however, took a proactive position and generated a CIA conspiracy to kill the president, a conspiracy that was hatched in the decadence of New Orleans' French Quarter.

It seems Lee Harvey Oswald spent some of his formative years here and was remembered for attempting to garner support for his Cuban sympathies. After Oswald's alleged (who really knows for sure) murder of the president, and subsequent death, Garrison linked him to a prominent Orleanian named Clay Shaw. This tenuous link was established by the fact that Oswald was once arrested for distributing subversive flyers outside the International Trade Mart, of which Shaw was the director.

In 1967, Shaw was indicted and arrested. In 1969 he was taken to trial. The star witness was Perry Russo, who recalled, under hypnosis, when the doses of sodium pentothal proved powerless, that Shaw, Oswald, and others were overheard discussing the conspiracy at the home of a well-known eccentric, David Ferrie. The other witnesses were a New York accountant who heard voices and routinely fingerprinted his daughter when she came home from college to make sure she had not been replaced by an imposter, and a most reputable junkie.

On March 1, 1969, the jury acquitted Shaw by a 10 to 2 vote. Garrison, we might add, seemed quite pleased that two members of the jury believed his theory. In the face of such a crushing defeat, Garrison took a day off and on March 3 charged Shaw with perjury. The federal government had apparently had quite enough of Garrison's shenanigans and enjoined the prosecution from proceeding.

Clay Shaw was physically, financially, and socially ruined by the ordeal. He died of lung cancer in 1974. Jim Garrison was elected to the Louisiana Court of Appeal, where he served for 13 years. He died in 1992. Russo made the news once again in 1993 when he rescued a crime victim in the French Quarter.

If you've read this far, you must have some interest in the subject and may want to read Jim Garrison's memoirs of the event, titled *On the Trail of the Assassins*. And if you'd like to trail the assassin on your own, you may want to take *Half-Shell's* Assassination Tour.

1313 Dauphine St. Clay Shaw's home

Tortorici's Restaurant 441 Royal—Garrison hung out and received much of his information here

700 block of Governor Nicholls Street Plaque commemorating Clay Shaw

Tulane and Broad streets The Criminal Court Building, where Judge Edward Haggerty presided over the trial of Clay Shaw in Section C

The World Trade Center Canal and the River—Clay Shaw was director and Lee Harvey Oswald was arrested for distributing flyers outside

3330 Louisiana Avenue Pkwy. David Ferrie's apartment, where the assassination plot was allegedly concocted

Beauregard Junior High 4621 Canal—Lee Harvey Oswald matriculated here

OTHER BOOKS OF INTEREST

Plot or Politics: The Garrison Case and Its Cast by Rosemary James and Jack Wardlaw; contact Pelican Publishing Company

American Grotesque by James Kirkwood

HE MUST HAVE SOMETHING

You bet he does. And what he has is the real/true story of the Garrison assassination probe. Stephen Tyler, a New Orleans

---

THE RICH AND FAMOUS

Everybody's fantasy is to have enough money to buy a vacation/alternate home in some exotic locale. What could be more exotic than New Orleans? At least that appears to be the attitude of the many celebs who have been purchasing New Orleans real estate with gold-rush fervor. Robin Leach could do a whole season and not leave the French Quarter except to venture Uptown to Bob Dylan's palatial hideaway.

Director Taylor Hackford and his wife, actress Helen Mirren, have been residents for several years. Gerald McRaney and Delta Burke are just a few blocks from the Francis Ford Coppolas. Daniel Lanois, music producer extraordinaire, *has a house and studio on Esplanade and Peter Buck, of the group REM, has taken up residence on Burgundy. The noted patron of the arts Frederick Weismann maintains a restored town house on St. Philip Street.*

There are, of course, many others who reside at least part time here in the Crescent City. (That's what they used to call us before that dreadful movie with Dennis Quaid hit theaters.) If you want to know more, read Betty Gillaud's column in The Times-Picayune. *Who else would tell you these things?*

independent producer, took a quote from one of Shaw's incredulous defense attorneys to title his documentary film, *He Must Have Something*. In addition to what is probably the last recorded interview that Jim Garrison ever gave, Tyler interviewed all the key players who were still living in 1991-92. The talking heads included the presiding judge and his court reporter, Perry Russo, attorneys for both the defense and prosecution, and reporters who covered the debacle.

After viewing *He Must Have Something*, one might conclude that there was absolutely no substance to the theory that Clay Shaw was involved in a conspiracy to assassinate John F. Kennedy. Aside from that, who really knows. Lee Harvey Oswald spent time in New Orleans. He had enough sympathy with Castro to risk ridicule and arrest by distributing propaganda in downtown New Orleans. Kennedy orchestrated the Bay of Pigs invasion. There are many bays in the area, not to mention lakes, bayous, and drainage ditches. Pigs are equally abundant, both four legged and porkers who walk upright. Hmmm . . . maybe he did have something.

For the best academic take on Garrison, visit Michael Kurtz, a professor at Southeastern Louisiana University in Hammond and one of the first recipients of the Zapruder film, sent to him by Garrison.

Notable Moments in New Orleans Film

Woody Allen's *Crimes and Misdemeanors* got a huge laugh from local audiences with the line about the hit man being back in New Orleans.

After their big score in *Easy Rider*, Captain America and Billy headed for Mardi Gras, as did most everyone else in almost every other movie ever made about our fair metropolis.

Finally, and again, completely arbitrarily, the worst movie ever made in and about New Orleans had to do with a swarm of killer bees heading north from South America. Their ETA coincidentally coincided with the carnival season. The day was saved when the swarm attacked a Volkswagen, which was then driven into the Superdome, where the air-conditioning system was lowered to a temperature that would immobilize the bees so that they could be safely exterminated. The city was saved and the parades rolled on schedule. Whew!

The Independents

New Orleans is not dependent on outsiders for film productions. There is a small but talented group of independent filmmakers who call the Crescent City home.

Stevenson Palfi is the video documentarian who made the critically acclaimed *Piano Players Rarely Ever Play Together.* This feature has been shown often on cable TV's Bravo channel, and chronicles the events leading up to a concert featuring three of New Orleans' finest piano players: Professor Longhair, Tuts Washington, and Allen Toussaint. Before the actual performance could take place, da Professa' passed away and the film took on a new significance, documenting the final performances and funeral of a musical legend. Other Palfi productions include a one-man performance by actor John O'Neil called *Don't Start Me Talkin'*, and a documentary on Papa John Creech.

Stephen Tyler is a writer/director with a keen ear for dialogue and a scholarly approach to film direction.

Neil Alexander is a still photographer and video documentarian who captures the nuances of life in the Crescent City.

Karen Snyder is another independent whose efforts have chronicled the New Orleans tradition of stoop sitting and the history of the St. Charles Avenue streetcar.

Wanna make your own movies? Then go see the good folks at the New Orleans Video Access Center, or "NOVAC," as we know it. NOVAC has the facilities, equipment, and expertise to help the beginner turn a good idea into a production. They can also help you get it on TV by way of the community access channels.

NOVAC 2010 Magazine St. (524-8626)

Commercial Cinema

The outlets for conventional Hollywood movies are similar to those in other cities, with multiscreen suburban cinemas dominating the market. However, for something a *little* different, try:

Prytania Theatre 5339 Prytania (895-4513) A real treat.

Loyola Film Buffs Institute (865-3146) This series focuses on foreign and American classics, both old and new. As the name implies, for serious cinephiles, but also for those merely in pursuit of pleasure.

Tulane University Cinema (865-5143) Another campus film series, but lacking the serious intent of the Loyola series.

Canal Place Cinema 1 Canal Place (foot of Canal Street) (581-5400) The most unconventional conventional movie house is the Canal Place Cinema. The design of the theater itself is architecturally pleasing and the slate of films usually includes the avant-garde and foreign fare.

Galleria Cinemas 1 Galleria Blvd., Metairie (838-8356) The Galleria Cinemas also occasionally devote a screen to art films. The parking here is plentiful in the high-rise lot, but at peak hours go early to avoid having to navigate the masses.

Movie Pitchers 3941 Bienville (488-8881) A multi-, small-screen cinema that features second-run and art films. Each theater is set up with tables, cabaret style, and some theater seats. Beer and food are sold for consumption during the screening. Movie Pitchers also hosts plays and stand-up comedy.

For a cheap evening out, there are many dollar cinemas in town. The thing to remember is that almost everyone has a dollar, and dropping the kids off for a couple of hours is cheaper than paying a baby-sitter.

Recreation

New Orleans residents and visitors are abundantly blessed with a myriad of available activities. From the zoo and picnicking to the Saints and sailing, we've got it all! The time has arrived to take an excursion into a potpourri of recreational opportunities that are bound to satisfy your hunt for suitable diversions.

Nature at Its Best

When the last song is sung and the last toast is drunk, where can you go to get away from it all? Not to worry, stranger—you won't even have time to see all of the parks we've got.

Audubon Park Named for John James himself, Audubon Park is a bird sanctuary that also provides humans with a haven from the hustle and bustle of urban pressure. The

location is Uptown, sandwiched between St. Charles Avenue and the Mississippi River. Driving on St. Charles past stately mansions and Tulane and Loyola universities is worth the journey to Audubon Park alone. Sprawling oak trees draped with Spanish moss form a picturesque canopy for much of the park. Home of the Audubon Zoo, horseback riding, golf, picnicking, soccer fields, Riverview (the area behind the levee), and the finish line of the Crescent City Classic footrace, Audubon Park offers something for all ages and is a must on the list of family outings.

City Park City Park is one of the city's major play and escape areas. With lazy lagoons and thousands of oak trees, City Park provides therapeutic benefits for stressed citizens. Storyland, boating, fishing, an amusement park with an antique carousel, the miniature train, and the puppet shows provide fun-filled hours for even the most insatiable children. Adults are well served by 40 tennis courts, numerous ball fields, botanical gardens, a lighted golf driving range, and four 18-hole golf courses. The New Orleans Museum of Art is in the park, houses both permanent and visiting treasures, and is well worth the price of museum admission. Hundreds of WPA depression-era bridges, fountains, and statues are scattered throughout the park and provide perhaps the world's largest outdoor museum. City Park is a wonderful getaway for a lunch hour or a family reunion.

Armstrong Park Named after the most famous of New Orleans jazz musicians, this downtown park is located on Rampart Street and includes the Municipal Auditorium, the Theatre of the Performing Arts, and Congo Square. Lagoons and bridges accent the restored 19th-century buildings. Armstrong Park is the scene of many of the city's cultural events. One wonders how old Satchmo would feel if he knew his neighborhood had been bulldozed to build a park in his honor. (Caution should be exercised after dark.)

Lakefront On the north end of City Park, Lakeshore Drive follows the shoreline of Lake Pontchartrain from West End to beyond the University of New Orleans and the Industrial

Canal. A seawall and levee follow the winding drive that is dotted with benches, picnic tables, and playgrounds. Thousands of natives swamp the Lakefront during spring and summer, but it is relatively deserted at other times (and occasionally deserted even on weekends). By the way, *don't swim* in the lake. Urban runoff has taken its toll, but reclamation is under way. We recommend sunbathing, sunsets, and the continuation of the Lakefront's unofficial designation as the historic make-out area of New Orleans.

Lafreniere Park Situated on the site of the old Jefferson Downs racetrack in suburban Metairie, Lafreniere Park is an island refuge in the midst of the concrete and neon nightmare that is Veterans Highway. Beautifully laid out with lagoons, fountains, pedestrian bridges, and a small lake, this green space provides a necessary getaway for many. A jogging/walking trail, paddle boats, playgrounds, ball fields, and ample parking make this park #1 on the east bank of Jefferson. The island houses a welcome pavilion in the middle of the lake and provides some of the only shade in this park. In 20 years or so, the younger trees will grow to make this area a perfect place for all-day summer picnics. Right now it's fine for late-afternoon activities and family excursions, but too hot during midday in the summer.

Bayou Segnette State Park What other city offers the chance to stay in a picturesque swamp cabin overlooking a bayou, and *only 20 minutes* from downtown? This is a natural park setting that provides a taste of adventure among animal inhabitants and swampland vegetation. Whether for a short

---

FIVE FREE ROMANTIC SPOTS

1. The ruins of Spanish Fort along Bayou St. John
2. The hidden and oft-forgotten Popps Fountain in City Park
3. Along Lakeshore Drive at sunset
4. Among the oaks at Audubon or City Park
5. A late-night ferry ride over the river and back

outing or several nights, this state park is highly recommended and the distance can't be beat. Bayou Segnette State
Park is located in Westwego just off the Westbank Expressway
(U.S. 90) across the Mississippi River (436-1107). By the way,
don't forget the insect repellent.

Jean Lafitte National Historical Park (Barataria Unit) Imagine nearly 9,000 acres of Louisiana's swamp and marsh wetlands, teeming with alligators, snakes, deer, nutrias (basically
muskrats on steroids), and untold numbers of birds and
plants. Just 30 minutes from downtown, this park provides
easy access to another world. Take the Crescent City Connection to the Westbank Expressway (U.S. 90) and turn left
at Barataria Boulevard (Hwy. 45). Take 45 for 7 miles to the
park entrance. Voila!

Fort Pike State Commemorative Area This is a historic fort
built in 1827 as a waterway defense to the city. Take the Chef
(U.S. 90) east past French Camp several miles. You can't miss
it. This route is also a good alternative to taking I-10 every
time you leave the city. Rest rooms and facilities for picnics
are available. Mosquitoes are normally of the mammoth

The Levee

variety—bug spray time again. But don't let that deter you from this exciting excursion. Remember, the mosquito is our state bird, not the pelican as you thought.

Nature—The Sequel—For those who prefer their outdoors to be a bit more prepackaged, we offer the following classics:

Audubon Zoo (861-2537) Consistently rated as a "top 10 zoo" in the United States, the Audubon Zoo has something for everyone in as natural a setting as one can expect (of course, the animals may have a different view on this, but since when have we asked them?). The habitats have been constructed with zoological authenticity and are well maintained for the 1,500 animals that inhabit the zoo's 60 lush, beautiful acres. The Reptile Encounter, Pathways to the Past, the Wisner Children's Village, and the Louisiana Swamp Exhibit are but a few highlights that make Audubon an A-plus zoo.

For lagniappe, take the riverboat from the French Quarter to the zoo and back, or the streetcar, where free shuttle service is provided from streetcar stop #36. Top that one, San Diego or D.C.! The Audubon Zoo is located in Audubon Park at 6500 Magazine St. If you're going to drive, taking St. Charles Avenue to the park is more fun, faster, and will produce less tension through fewer potholes than the Magazine street route, but the riverboat or streetcar is by far the best experience. Getting there is half the fun. Open 7 days.

Louisiana Nature Center (246-5672) Larger than the zoo, the Nature Center offers an unusual closeup view of Louisiana's native plants and animals (and we're not talking about the 9th Ward). Exhibits, boardwalks, several nature trails, and other features provide wildlife viewing and give visitors a rare glimpse of the state's natural environment without leaving the urban area. The planetarium, gift shop, and multimedia shows are real bonuses.

As you exit the Nature Center, you may be startled by the concrete-and-steel contrast unsuitably dubbed Lake Forest Shopping Mall, where one may purchase books reminding us of the delicacy of the ecosystem.

The Nature Center is located in New Orleans East at Joe

Brown Memorial Park, 5601 Read Blvd. (take I-10 East from downtown to the Read exit).

Aquarium of the Americas The Aquarium is the major spectacle at the new Woldenberg Riverfront Park. Encompassing 16 acres, this park has been the focus of widespread community effort and support (now if we can only achieve this level of enthusiasm for the orchestra year after year). The Mississippi Riverfront downtown is the proper setting for this waterfront park. Five natural aquatic habitats, including the Caribbean Reef and Amazon exhibits, complement our local flavor of the River, the Delta, and the Gulf. Many other exhibits will enthrall you, as well. The restaurant overlooking the Mississippi provides a delightful view.

Participatory Activities

If our natural attractions just can't provide the thrills you desire, then the following is all for you, jocko. We also suggest checking the Calendar section of the daily newspaper, as well as the Sports section for updates and listings. The Wednesday paper provides a special Sports/Activity section, too.

RUNNING AND ROAD RACING

Scenic running and jogging paths abound: Lakeshore Drive, City Park, Audubon Park, levees, neutral grounds (the medians on the main streets), and dodging streetcars on the tracks of St. Charles Avenue. East Jefferson Parish provides a marvelous multimile asphalt path that runs from Bucktown to Kenner.

The premier road race in New Orleans for spectators and participants is the **Crescent City Classic**, now spanning three decades. The Classic is a TAC-approved 10,000-meter (6.2 miles) excuse for a terrific party. You can race, run, jog, or walk this spring event. It has emerged as one of the top 10K races in the nation since it sports a flat course and is conducive to world records (the Classic was the home of the 10K world record by Mark Nenow for many years).

But do not be awed by this. Anyone can participate and

should, if he or she likes to party. We have run this race ourselves amidst the throngs (close to 35,000 runners at last count). Unless you are a world-class runner, do not plan on setting a personal best in the Crescent City Classic. Here's why: the race/party begins in the French Quarter with runners in costumes, makeup, on stilts and skates, and, yes, we have seen topless participants (mostly men). The thousands of runners are backed up through the Quarter for many blocks, and by the time the last partygoers reach the starting line in front of Jackson Square, the first of the international racing stars is crossing the finish line. *Comprendez?* The course takes you through the Central Business District, and as you wind down residentially elegant Prytania Street, perhaps a stop for a Bloody Mary at one of the many wateringholes along the way would be in order. In addition to the gracious offerings of refreshing showers from water hoses, many residents provide cups of water, Gatorade, and even champagne as you exit the beautiful treelined street and enter the final lap in Audubon Park.

The race ends at the Mississippi River and the festival begins. Your entry fee (modest) provides you with the traditional T-shirt, but also all of the fruit, beer, jambalaya, and spring water you can absorb. Now enjoy the picnic atmosphere of the remainder of the day as you relax to the music of some of New Orleans' favorite bands. Free bus transportation back to the French Quarter is available, but for a real treat, take the riverboat.

The Crescent City Classic is no longer just a race. It has become a Happening to enjoy either as a partaker or spectator. Look for publicity at running-shoe stores and in the newspaper after January. Don't forget to purchase a collector's poster, signed and numbered.

The **Greater New Orleans Runners Association** is an organization of several thousand runners and walkers. Information on races: 6112 Magazine (899-3333)

Founded in 1963, the **New Orleans Track Club** is the granddaddy of running clubs and attracts not only runners but also walkers and wheelchair athletes. (482-6682)

BOWLING

Bowling alleys were once looked upon as the domain of the Archie Bunkers of the world. Then someone discovered that those blue-collar keglers were having fun, and the local haute monde began to take up the sport themselves. However, the crowd is not headed to the suburbs to one of those highly automated, multilane extravaganzas; it's going to the **Mid-City Bowling Lanes and Sports Palace**.

Mid-City Lanes still has the classic pink Brunswick pinspotters, circa '67, and you have to keep your own score, which is probably a lost art. But while the ceiling fans stir the air and you try to pick up a spare on the 7-10 split, you can feast on John Blancher's tasty fried alligator platter or shake your groove thing to the live bands that play on the weekends. College students take their dates, parents take their kids, and even a few serious bowlers show up on occasion. 4133 S. Carrollton Ave. near Tulane Ave. (482-3133). See **Music.**

> **Paradise Bowling Lanes** 3717 Veterans Blvd. (888-4141)
> **Bowlarama** 1008 Jefferson Hwy. (833-5568)
> **New Orleans Bowling Association** (482-2272)
> **New Orleans Women's Bowling Association** (486-3031)

LEAGUE SPORTS

Literally hundreds of opportunities exist to play league sports in the Greater New Orleans area. Check the sports pages for the most complete and up-to-date information for seasonal sports leagues. A quick telephone call to recreation departments, parks, and playgrounds will provide you with contacts. Your friendly neighborhood tavern usually sponsors a team or two as well.

We have named a few here that present something other than the ordinary:

> **Calypso Women's Soccer Club** (866-5586) A competitive soccer organization for females.
> **Lafreniere Women's Soccer Club** (466-0441) Social and competitive soccer for females ages 14-40.

New Orleans Rugby Football Club (947-2048) or (887-2998) A renowned club participating in tournaments throughout the nation. New members welcomed.

New Orleans Women's Rugby Club (486-4229) or (947-5498) A competitive women's athletic club. You do not have to have experience in rugby.

GNO Athletic League (393-9608) Corporate athletic competition.

Over 40 Baseball League (887-8752) For those of you who have survived the bottom 40 and are headed for the top 40.

TENNIS

Several parks offer public tennis courts through reservations:

City Park (483-9383) 40 lighted rubico and laykold courts. The Wisner Tennis Center at City Park offers tennis instruction, racquet repair, and a pro shop.

Audubon Park (895-1042) 10 unlighted clay courts. No pro shop, but instruction is available, and according to our information from the park, "the clientele here is beautiful!" We are not certain as to the meaning and definitely are not going to be responsible for the interpretation of this statement, but we are investigating daily.

Metro Tennis League (643-7121) or (246-1084) Boasting nearly 1,500 members from over 30 area tennis groups. Promotes amateur competition and social events for members.

WRIGLEY FIELD SOUTH

Not being baseball fans, we're hard-pressed to figure out why many New Orleanians are rabid fans of the Chicago Cubs. When the springtime rolls around, the fans of those Cubbies return to the bleachers at the Milan Lounge with the regularity of the swallows at Capistrano. There they cheer on their favorite Boys of Summer while surrounded by others with the same affliction. **Milan Lounge** *1312 Milan St. (just off Prytania) (895-1836)*

Many playgrounds and parks in the Greater New Orleans area provide one or more courts as well. For information on a location near you, telephone NORD Tennis Center at 896-4747 or Jefferson Parish Athletic Division at 736-6999.

GOLF

Each spring the Freeport McMoRan Golf Classic is held in New Orleans at English Turn golf course. Available for public recreation are:

City Park (483-9397) Four 18-hole courses are available, with a pro shop, restaurants, and cart rentals, plus a double-decker driving range.

Audubon Park (865-8260) A small but beautiful course Uptown amid the oaks.

Pontchartrain Park (288-0928)

Brechtel Park Municipal Golf Course (362-4761)
                            Driving Range (367-9054)

BICYCLING

Crescent City Cyclists (486-3683) A bicycle touring group of over 500 members.

French Quarter—**Bicycle Michael's** 618 Frenchmen St. (945-9505) Rentals.

CRABBIN'

If you're not from these parts, you probably never considered that there could be anything desirable about catching crabs. One of the good things about Lake Pontchartrain is that these crustaceans are thriving in the lake's murky waters. Lake Pontchartrain crabs are considered to be the best the area's waters have to offer. All it takes are a few inexpensive nets, which can be purchased at most sporting-goods stores, and some chicken necks or other meat scraps for bait. Kick back, relax, check the nets every 15 minutes, and if you're lucky, you can go home with enough crabs to boil for dinner.

Mid-City—**Joe's Bicycle** 2501 Tulane Ave. (close to Dixie Brewery) (821-2350) Rentals.

Uptown—**Bikesmith** 4716 Freret St. (899-8356)

BOATING

Lake Pontchartrain provides boaters with an ideal location adjacent to the city. Sailing and powerboat opportunities are many and varied and offered year round. Nearby bayous and waterways provide an expansive array of excursion and charter adventures.

Paddle Boats, Skiffs, Canoes City Park, Lafreniere Park

Flipper Too (888-4882) Fishing charter.

New Orleans Rowing Club (895-0425) or (522-3731) Promoting rowing, both competitive and recreational.

Lake Pontchartrain Hunter Fleet (888-6948) or (282-3880) Sailing.

New Orleans Venture Club (886-4544) or (347-8622) Sailing.

DIVING

Diving trips are arranged through several nationally certified diving schools and dive shops. These include oil-rig dives and normally require a substantial outlay of pesos. (Isn't the SCUBA-diving industry interesting? Imagine purchasing your driver's license and driving instruction from the same auto

---

GAMBLING

There has always been gambling in New Orleans. In the past, there were pinball machines, racetracks, and bingo games. Now we have other, more serious, forms of gambling. The Las Vegas nature of these new riverboats and casinos is so at odds with the low-key charm of our city that this is the extent of our acknowledgment of the new gambling scene.

dealer that sells you your new car and maintains it. Conflict of interest or what!? That's how the industry works. Good luck.)

Harry's Dive Shop (NAUI) 4709 Airline Hwy. (888-4882)

Aqua Tech Dive Center (PADI) 6101 Westbank Expwy. (341-DIVE)

Sirens Dive Club (241-2390) Forget your antidiscrimination laws; this dive club is for females only.

HORSEBACK RIDING

Yes, right here in the city you can rent horses and practice your equestrian skills. And you don't have to go all the way out to the popular stables in Picayune, Miss., to ride.

Audubon Park Stables (897-2817)

Brittany Stables 12401 Curran Blvd. (241-9746)

Cascade Stables 6500 Magazine St. (891-2246)

Cajun Rangers Riding Club (245-9123) Join and you'll have the opportunity to ride your horse in a Mardi Gras parade.

SKATING RINKS

Skateland 1019 Charbonnet (947-2079)

Skate Country 6711 Airline (733-2248)

W.B. Skate Country 1100 Terry Pkwy., Gretna (392-2227) That's "W.B." for "West Bank," of course.

BINGO

You could probably walk right into any of the dozens of charitable- and religious-organization bingo games around the city. They routinely fly a conspicuous banner advertising the event located between the statue of Jesus and the sign with Sunday's schedule of church services. But if you want bingo with the emphasis on deluxe, then it's the Napoleon Room in Metairie for you! Offering two—count 'em—two nightly sessions, security, and a great food menu. Why, not even Josephine could ask for more. Located at 4631 W. Napoleon (where else?). (454-8193)

BILLIARD PARLORS

OK, OK—pool halls, and we've still got some good ones that have been around a long time. Oftentimes you'll find quality food there as well. Here are a couple of recommendations. (Sorry, we don't recommend any pool halls where bikers hang out. We're not into leather jackets or the risk of physical harm.)

Whitey's Pool Hall 3764 Derbigny (833-9122) A classic.

Sport Palace 1125 Jefferson Hwy. (835-9117) Check it out: open 24 hours and serving up some pretty good boiled seafood.

Big Easy Billiards & Sports Bar 1200 S. Clearview (733-2783)

Whitey's Pool Hall 4314 Downman Rd. (241-2893) Another classic across town from its Metairie cousin. Boiled crawfish, crabs, and shrimp.

DANCING

Many of you delight to tripping the lights fantastic, and here is a really unusual array. No Arthur Murray in this book!

Jamaica Dance Club (738-3092) or (469-4677) A group dedicated to the preservation of the dance called "Jamaica" by teaching and dancing since 1962.

Caledonian Scottish Dancers (866-2220) Grab your family tartan and take lessons in Scottish folk dancing. Perhaps you'll be asked to lead in the next production of *Brigadoon*.

New Orleans International Folkdance Group (455-5678) Recreational folkdance and a chance to perform at local festivals.

Mardi Gras Dancers (837-0672) Cajun dancing from down da bayou.

MASKING AND COSTUMES

With the festivals, Halloween, and Mardi Gras, you will certainly want to participate in masking on these occasions. Bring the kids in, too!

Almost New Clothing 2005 Magazine (522-8355) Some economical buys here with resale costumes.

Jo-Ann Costume 1732 Dryades (523-1788) or 3118 Severn (885-4328) Disguising New Orleanians for over half a century.

Costume Headquarters 240 Iris (488-9523) Rentals as well as purchases.

Exits & Entrances 1617 St. Charles (581-3999) We can't vouch for this place, but we wanted to include it because the name is almost as clever as the title of our book.

Vieux Carre Hair Store 805 Royal (522-3258) Probably the oldest costume and makeup shop in the city.

MORE PARTICIPATORY ACTIVITIES— AN ESOTERIC LISTING

Go fly a kite! That's right—with the **Crescent City Kiteflyers** (529-3247).

And how about George Bush's favorite lawn sport: **Horseshoe Pitchers Association** (737-9959) has 160 members competing in leagues and tournaments.

Triangle West Bar Dart Club (737-9083) sponsors league and tournament play.

Bicycle Polo Clubs have grown to three: (866-6703), (895-7323), and (488-1946).

Ultimate Frisbee (943-1944) recruits new members for tournaments.

The Trampoline Jump Center has welcomed adults and youth for decades. 1620 Veterans Hwy. (834-1591).

We figured esoteric participatory activities was the right category for **Indian Hills Nudist Park** (641-9998).

Spectator Sports

Go Saints Go

What other team in the annals of professional football can boast of full stadiums for over two decades despite only a few winning seasons? New Orleans loves the Saints. Names like Danny Abramowicz, John Gilliam, and the beloved Archie Manning will live on in our memories forever. Yes, they played for the Saints, right along with the Snake, the Wheel, the Flea, and of course Moses, better known as Charlton Heston. That's right—the actor even had an infamous role with the Saints in one of his least memorable performances.

A Saints game in the Superdome is a real party in itself, win or lose. Arrive about two or three hours early in the vicinity of the Dome. Bars in the area usually have buffets or game-day specials, and the prices are reasonable. The adjoining Hyatt Hotel lobby and mall areas provide an exciting bit of merriment to rev you up for kickoff. There are constant impromptu pep rallies, music, dancing, and fabulous people-watching opportunities. So put on your black and gold and boogie down to the Superdome. Who dat?! Who dat?! Who dat say dey gon' beat dem Saints?! Who dat?!

SUPERDOME

The large flying-saucer-shaped building near the interstate highway close to downtown is the Superdome. America's largest indoor stadium is an excellent sports facility, but true to Louisiana tradition, the Dome has been surrounded by controversy since its inception. Originally designed to cost $63 million, the actual cost was closer to $167 million. It is well worth a visit if the opportunity arises. It plays host to the Super Bowls, Tulane, the Saints, and the Sugar Bowl.

Minor-League Baseball

New Orleans now boasts its own minor-league (AAA) team, the Zephyrs, farm team for the Milwaukee Brewers. There are 72 games from April through September, with the home games being played at the UNO campus. For tickets or information, call 282-6777.

Professional Soccer

The New Orleans Gamblers (244-7267) are the equivalent of a European third-division team. You can catch them in action in the spring and summer at Pan-American Stadium in City Park, usually on Saturday nights, although the times vary.

College Sports

Tulane University and the University of New Orleans compete in Division I NCAA sports. Tulane plays football in the Superdome against potent teams from throughout the nation and occasionally upsets a major power (hopefully LSU).

Any baseball game on UNO's lakefront has a real laid-back sports flavor, even for New Orleans, but the annual Pelican Cup Baseball Series between Tulane and UNO has developed into quite a rivalry. UNO has emerged as a perennial college baseball power and normally is nationally ranked. UNO has a better baseball team than Tulane (the authors both graduated from UNO).

At the beginning of each college baseball season, the Superdome is the scene for some real, major-power, college baseball. It's the Louisiana v. Florida or California or Oklahoma Weekend Series. This sensational event pits the best baseball teams in the state (usually LSU, UNO, and Tulane) against the best of another state, and is well worth the price of admission for baseball enthusiasts.

Tulane and UNO also have basketball programs that are noteworthy. UNO plays in the magnificent Lakefront Arena. Xavier University, Southern University at New Orleans, and Delgado Community College offer sports programs throughout the year. Check the newspaper or telephone the athletic office of any of the New Orleans area colleges and universities for schedules and complete information.

NCAA NATIONAL FLAG FOOTBALL CHAMPIONSHIP

During Sugar Bowl week, just prior to New Year's, the University of New Orleans plays host to the NCAA National Flag Football Championship. This sports event has grown from a handful of local and state teams to a premier athletic competition hosting over 100 teams from throughout the nation. If your college does not already participate, then it's time to contact your alma mater. There's no better way to take in New Orleans than during this time of the year, when the city really rocks. Anytime in the Quarter is the right time, but on New Year's Eve the district vibrates with jovial diversity.

SUGAR BOWL

This, of course, is the sweetest of bowl games and (formerly) annually pitted the champion of the Southeastern Conference, the toughest of all conferences, against a national contender. In 1995, the Sugar began to be in the rotation for the national championship. For football at its best, plan on this New Year's game.

THE BAYOU CLASSIC

This is an annual football event held in the Dome featuring the magnificent marching bands of Grambling and Southern. If you have never had the pleasure of witnessing the spectacle of the Grambling band, then you should attend this show f'sure. Oh yes, the football rivalry between these two schools is fierce, and Eddie Robinson's Grambling Tigers are as legendary as college football ever becomes. Normally held in November.

High-School Football Finals

One would think that high-school teams would be awestruck playing in the Dome, but such is not the case. At the end of every football season the final championship game is held in the Superdome for each level of student population class (1, 2, 3, 4A, and 5).

And Speaking of the Superdome and Spectator Sports

Through the years the Superdome has played host to Super Bowls, Final Fours, and World Heavyweight Boxing championships. In addition, the Dome provides year-round sports entertainment, with regular billings of Supercross, soccer, exhibition pro baseball, truck and tractor pulls, boat shows, and sportsmen shows. Call 587-3810 for a schedule of events.

Horse Racing

New Orleans is blessed with the third oldest racetrack in the nation. The Fair Grounds, rising from the ashes after a disastrous fire, offers 101 days of Thoroughbred racing that begins on Thanksgiving Day. For a taste of the best that we can provide, try treating yourself to an experience at the Fair Grounds on opening day. Located on Gentilly Boulevard. (944-5515)

HEY, JUDE!

If your pursuits of happiness lean toward the cerebral and your idea of fun is to outwit an adversary, you should visit Jude Acers at his place of business at the French Market. Jude is a senior master of the chessboard and on most days has three boards set up and ready to take on all challengers, one at a time or three at once. For a mere $5 you can test your prowess against a man who once held the record for playing the most opponents at one time (179). His enterprise is located just downriver from St. Philip Street on Decatur and he accepts cash and credit cards. Look for his trademark red beret.

Tours

You want tours? We got tours. But you won't find any of the stuffy, canned sight-seeing tours in our recommendations. If those are what you want, check the Yellow Pages for the generic, chain-store tour lines.

City Tours

The Greater New Orleans Tourist and Convention Commission (what a mouthful) offers a treasure of brochures on the city. One that we like in particular outlines self-guided tours like the two below.

NEW ORLEANS DRIVING TOUR

This takes approximately three hours and includes 36 numbered major and minor sights. May we suggest the following possibilities for dining during your tour (all casual):

LOOK UP

When you're walking or driving around town, especially in the commercial areas of Canal Street, the Quarter, and Magazine Street, pry your eyes from those display windows and look up. You'll see some very fine historical architecture that contributes significantly to New Orleans' sense of place. On Canal Street, for example, the men's clothing store at the corner of St. Charles and Canal is housed in a series of four historic landmarks built in the 1850s. At the corner of Canal and Camp is a five-story Italianate building built around 1860. If your sense of aesthetics is dulled by all this fine 19th-century architecture, you need only contrast these with the abomination known as the San Lin Building, in the 500 block of Canal. (The owner's daughters are named Sandra and Linda.)

#8 Bud's Broiler for burgers (City Park Avenue)

#11 Sid-Mar's (1824 Orpheum) or **R&O's** (1210 Old Hammond Hwy.) for seafood or po' boys

Marina Grill for a burger and onion mum (Lake Marina Avenue)

#13 College Inn for lunch specials and po' boys (3016 S. Carrollton)

#14 Camellia Grill for omelets and burgers (626 S. Carrollton)

#20 Parasol's for po' boys and specials (2533 Constance)

FRENCH QUARTER WALKING TOUR

Allow three or more hours for this tour, depending on your pace and interests. There are dozens of great places to eat in the Quarter, so see our **Food** chapter for suggestions.

For your copy of a self-guided tour brochure, call the GNO Tourist and Convention Commission at (504) 566-5031, or visit in the Quarter at 529 St. Ann St.

National Park Service Tours

It is difficult to imagine the French Quarter as a National Historical Park, but it has indeed been designated just that— the French Quarter Unit of Jean Lafitte National Historical Park—with rangers in uniform even! A fact that should become

---

FLEA MARKET

The Flea Market is located at the end of the French Market at Barracks and French Market Place. The Flea Market is in operation on Saturdays and Sundays and in a limited capacity on weekdays. This is a great place to buy just about anything you can imagine and also just to people watch. On a pleasant weekend afternoon the crowds are large and interesting. Be sure to purchase a sweet-potato pie from the Pie Man for a real treat!

more well known through the years is that free walking tours guided by park rangers are offered on a regular schedule. Tours begin at the Folklife and Visitor Center located at 916 N. Peters in the French Market (about two blocks from Jackson Square). Walks are escorted seven days a week except Mardi Gras, Christmas, and New Year's. Several varieties of tours are available and most are less than two hours in length. Highly recommended. (589-2636)

The three tours highlighted thus far in this section have two things in common: they are free and they are great tours. The following tours are highly recommended, but do charge an admission:

Bayou Segnette Swamp Boat Tour 502 Laroussini, Westwego (561-8244) Experience the swamp as its inhabitants do. Native Cajun boat captains.

Musicana Shrine and Church Tours 925 St. Louis (566-0999) A great family tour emphasizing history, art, and architecture.

Save Our Cemeteries (588-9357) Offers one-hour tours of Lafayette Cemetery in the Garden District (the cemetery is on the National Register).

Riverboat Tours The following riverboats offer both short and lengthy trips at a variety of costs on the river and/or bayous: *Natchez, Creole Queen, Cotton Blossom, Bayou Jean Lafitte,* and *Cajun Queen.* These riverboats dock between the French Quarter and the Riverwalk.

Swamp and Voodoo Tours 724 Dumaine in the French Quarter (523-7685) Conducted by a practitioner of voodoo from the Voodoo Museum (perhaps a descendant of Marie Laveau).

MOST ROMANTIC VIEW OF THE CITY:
Returning from Algiers via the ferry
(from the West Bank to the East), right after dusk

Le' Ob's Tours (288-3478) Features cemetery, black heritage, and children's tours.

Louisiana Superdome Tours (587-3810) A fabulous facility, empty or full. If you can't see an event there then a guided tour is a distant second-best way to view the largest indoor stadium in the world.

Derwent Tours (943-6182) Specializes in tours for visitors from overseas. Multilingual guides provide services in a dozen languages.

Friends of the Cabildo Tours (523-3939) These guided tours of the French Quarter are exceptional. This is a walking tour, so wear your cross-trainers.

Buggy Tours Horse-drawn carriage tours are highly recommended. Normally 30 minutes in length through the French Quarter, these tours feature a narration of New Orleans history, seasoned with a little fiction for color. Reserve your carriage in front of Jackson Square (Gay 90's and Old Quarter Tours are the best).

Cradle of Jazz Tours (897-2115) Retrace the steps of such legends as Buddy Bolden, King Oliver, and Jelly Roll Morton on this two-hour jazz history and landmark tour. Participants will walk through Congo Square, get a look at the remains of Storyville, etc.—and all to the sounds of vintage recordings.

BEST VIEW OF THE CITY:
Top of the Mart Lounge, Canal Street at the River

Free and Cheap Things to Do with Kids

Half-Shell Award: Ride the St. Charles Avenue streetcar end to end

Feed the ducks at City Park or Lafreniere Park

Attend Mardi Gras parades (February/March)

Watch the Crescent City Classic on Prytania Street

Catch the boat races at the Lakefront on spring and summer weekends

Stroll through the French Market produce stands (free unless you pick up a Creole tomato, which you probably should do)

Fish at City Park (dig your own worms)

Take advantage of free days and times at the museums

Ride the Hyatt Hotel glass elevator to the top (let the kids push the buttons)

Walk around Jackson Square and watch the clowns, mimes, and musicians

View the holiday lights at City Park's Celebration in the Oaks

Catch a cabbage at the St. Patrick's Day Parade (in the city or Metairie)

Drive by Al Copeland's Christmas display in Metairie

Watch a rugby game at Audubon Park Riverview

Visit a cemetery (in the daytime)

Identify passing ships at the Riverwalk or Moonwalk

Picnic at the Lakefront or at City or Audubon parks

Try the many fine playgrounds in Jefferson and New Orleans

Walk down the middle of Royal Street, where no cars are allowed during the day

Drive across the Huey P. Long Bridge and have the kids look down

Tour visiting military ships at Mardi Gras and New Year's

Half-Shell Award: Climb the massive oak trees at City and Audubon parks

Try the trampolines on Veterans Highway near Bonnabel

Visit free art galleries and shops in the French Quarter

THE BOYS IN THE BUBBLE

Out where West End and Pontchartrain boulevards intersect with Lakeshore Drive, Robert E. Lee, and Old Hammond Highway sits the famous New Orleans fallout shelter. This giant concrete dome was built during the cold war days of the early sixties and was to be the city's command post in time of attack. After the Red Menace became less threatening, it was maintained to function as the city's nerve center in the event of a serious hurricane.

Just to the rear of the shelter, on the city's widest neutral ground, stands a Celtic cross, a tribute to the thousands of Irishmen who died digging the New Basin Canal.

Count the pigeons that land on Andrew Jackson's statue at the Square

Volunteer to man water stations during road races

Walk into the St. Louis Cathedral, the oldest in the U.S.A., even if you're not Catholic—or religious

Watch the jets arrive at the New Orleans International Airport

Go Christmas caroling in Jackson Square

Stroll along the Riverwalk at the end of Poydras Street

Experience the Greek Festival held each May at the Hellenic Center on Bayou St. John

Watch the longshoremen unload ships at the docks

Observe praline making at Aunt Sally's in the Quarter

Watch beignet making at Cafe du Monde in the Riverwalk

Buy a snowball at the City Park stand by Marconi or at the Pavilion

Visit the public library regularly and get the kids library cards

Experience a St. Joseph's Day altar (ya gotta see this)

Drive north on River Road towards Gramercy on Christmas Eve to see the bonfires on the levee

For a spectacular night view of the city, drive over the Crescent City Connection or the I-10 Industrial Canal bridges

Tour *The Times-Picayune* newspaper plant

PRALINES

The praline ("prawleen") was a favorite candy in the area of Orléans, France, and the recipe immigrated to New Orleans with the Ursuline Nuns. It is a very sweet, disc-shaped candy made with sugar and pecans, and is something no visitor should fail to sample while here. The best pralines are made by my maw maw but you can make do with those from Evans or Aunt Sally's, which have their praline shops in the French Quarter near Jackson Square.

Drive the Kenner-La Place I-10 elevated route 15 miles through wetlands and swamp

Take some nets and chicken necks and go crabbing out Highway 90 in east New Orleans

Tour the Chalmette Battlefield and cemetery

Hike on the levee by Hayne Boulevard and check out the fishing camps

Catch the July 4 fireworks display at the River or Lakefront

Explore Spanish Fort at the Lake and Bayou St. John

Watch the yachts and sailboats come in at the Point on Lake Pontchartrain

Hike or bike the Bucktown-to-Kenner bike/pedestrian path along the Lake

Stand on the Bucktown pedestrian bridge in the afternoon and watch the boats and fishermen come in right under you with their catch

Read the Living section in the daily newspaper and Friday's Lagniappe section for free activities

Buy a King cake from McKenzie's and have a King cake party in January or February before Mardi Gras

Ride the train at City Park

Share a Lucky Dog (hot dog) from the portable vendors in the Quarter

Go to Storyland in City Park

Ride the Riverfront streetcar line

Take a bus ride from the French Quarter to the Lakefront or vice versa

Visit the hands-on Children's Museum at 428 Julia St.

See the history of New Orleans at the Musee Conti Wax Museum

Have chocolate milk and beignets at Morning Call or Cafe du Monde

Pick up a Sunday paper and Tastee donuts, and relax at the Lake in the early A.M. on the weekend

Ride the paddle boats at City Park and Lafreniere Park

Pick out something tacky and useless at the Flea Market in the Quarter

Share a muffuletta at Central Grocery

Go out for a lemon ice at Brocato's at 537 St. Ann or 214 N. Carrollton

Ride across the causeway on the longest bridge in the world to Fontainebleau State Park

---

SHOTGUN HOUSES

New Orleans displays many unique types of architecture; the shotgun house exemplifies the most common type of traditional home. The most popular shotgun is a two-family dwelling with a common wall running the length of the house and dividing it into two identical sides, each with its own front door. The shotgun house has three to seven rooms situated one after the other. It is so named because presumably one can stand at the front door, fire a shotgun, and the shot will pass through the house and out the back door without hitting anything. Please do not ask residents to prove this legendary fact, however!

Buy taffy from the mule-driven wagon of the Roman Candy Man

Take the Canal Street ferry to Old Algiers and back

Visit the Presbytere or Cabildo museums at Jackson Square

Take in the Carnival Museum at the old U.S. Mint

Ride the riverboat to the zoo and back (OK, so it's not so cheap, but a great deal!)

Attend an event or take a tour in the Superdome

Drive out to the Louisiana Nature Center

Go camping across the Lake

Have an artist draw a sketch of your kid(s) at Jackson Square

Forget McDonald's and share a burger at Camellia Grill

Journey to the Rivertown museums on Williams at the River in Kenner

---

BEST CANDY:
Roman Candy Man, at mule-drawn locations
and selected retail outlets for several generations

Yat Vernacular

A Yat is a New Orleans native who sounds as if he could be from Brooklyn. The name is derived from the regularly used phrase, "where yat?"—a popular form of greeting in New Orleans. When friends and acquaintances meet on the street, one will greet the other with, "Where yat?" The response is "Awright."

One local legend says that "where yat?" had its origin with jazz musicians, who greeted each other with the phrase, which meant "where are you playing tonight?" The exchange probably went: "Where yat, cap?" "Ova' by da Dew Drop, cap." And even if that's not the way it happened, it's a good story.

"Where Yat?" is also the title of a song by Bob O'Rourke that's performed by the Dukes of Dixieland, and which sort of explains the whole concept:

> "It's not 'hello,' or 'how are you,' or greetings such as that—
> In New Orleans, a friend is seen; we all say, 'where yat?'"

Some common Yat expressions are:

Where yat?: a greeting such as "How are you?" The appropriate response is "Awright."

Makin' groceries: doing the grocery shopping.

DON'T CALL IT "NEW ORLEENS"

It's true that we use that pronunciation for the names of the parish and the avenue, but if you use it as the name of the city you're instantly branded as an outsider. The name of the city is pronounced "New Orlunz," "New Awlins," "N'Awlins," or even "New Orleunz"; "New Oyunz" means you're from an old-line, Uptown family.

169

By my house: as in "he slept by my house last night." This translates as "he spent the night at my house."

Suck da haids: an expression that relates to the local practice of sucking the juice from the heads of boiled crawfish. While this may sound totally distasteful, it is actually very good.

Axe: ask. Don't panic if you're walking by some guys on the street and you overhear one tell the other, "Let's axe that dude." Hopefully they want the time or directions.

Ya mamma: reference to one's maternal parent: "How's ya mamma?"

Or what: to be included at the end of an interrogative sentence: "You goin' by ya mamma's, or what?"

Poppa Gator or Pop a Gator: a dance in which the participant proceeds to wallow on the floor. This usually occurs when the party is no longer under control.

Cap: not a head covering but the universal name for a male: "Hey cap, where ya headed?"

Charmer (pronounced "chawmah"): the female of the Yat species, whose favorite form of address is "dawlin."

Where ya stay at?: "Where do you live?"

Shurnuf: you got it!

Turlet: a receptacle for human waste.

Zinc: sink.

Erl: oil.

F'sure: for sure; an appropriate comment when in agreement; descendant of the sixties' "right on."

Berl: the method used for cooking crabs and crawfish.

Ersters: oysters.

Sure thing, sug: personable affirmative response.

Ohmagawd: Oh my God (pronounced rapidly).

Scuse me, poidan me: mannerly terms; both used in rapid succession.

I'll take me a . . .: may I have a . . .

Crawfish ball: crawfish boil.

Banquette (pronounced bankit): sidewalk.

Awright, hawt: female response of agreement.

Hey, how ya makin'?: "Hello, how are you?"

Over da riva: across the river.

Yeah, you right: the accent is on the first word and it's all pronounced as one. This is a sign of definite agreement.

Who dat's for?: those who do a better job with the King's English say, "Who is that for?" This phrase translates as "to whom does that belong?" and seeks to establish ownership.

Gris-Gris (Gree-Gree): a voodoo charm used to ward off evil spells, or to cast evil on one's enemies, such as the Los Angeles Rams. Also, the title of Dr. John's first solo album when he was known as the "Night Tripper."

For an outstanding exposé of Yats in action, read John Kennedy Toole's *A Confederacy of Dunces.*

A scholar of classical literature will be delighted to find streets named after the nine muses, but will be appalled at the local pronunciations:

Calliope=Cal/ee/ope

Melpomene=Mel/pa/meen

Terpsichore=Terp/si/core

Euterpe=U/terp

The old Clio Street streetcar was known as the "C-L ten"

THE PURPLE LADIES OF CANAL STREET

On most days, in the 700 block of Canal Street, just down the street from Woolworth's (or "Woolsworth," as it's known locally), the purple ladies set up their sidewalk outlet for brass jewelry, incense, crystals, exotic oils, and such. They are draped head to toe in purple, their table for their wares is covered in purple, and their van (of course, it's purple) is parked behind them. Besides their mystic penchant for purple, they also sport some of the most impressive dreadlocks this side of Kingston. Their store is next to Whole Foods Market in the Bayou St. John/Esplanade area. This fits in well with the Hare Krishna mansion just down the street.

Milan Street bears no resemblance to the Italian city and is pronounced My/lan

Many local terms are derived from French and have become part of the vernacular. Some of the more common terms are:

Marraine (Ma ran), **NaNan**, or **Nainanne** These are the Cajun French terms for a godmother, and **Parrain** (Pa ran) is the word for a godfather. The population of New Orleans is predominantly Catholic, and virtually everyone has a NaNan and Parrain. Dr. John's version of "Iko Iko" contains the verse, "My marraine told your marraine," etc.

Bayou This word is French by way of the Choctaw Indians. It is not peculiar to the New Orleans vocabulary, but it is frequently mispronounced. It is "by-you." We know Hank Williams, Sr., had big fun on the By Oh, but Hank was from Alabama.

Faubourg This is a French term meaning suburb or outlying area. Some of our inner city neighborhoods are the Faubourg Marigny and Faubourg St. John.

BEST YAT NAME:
Anna Mae, with "Nat'ly" a close second

Creole or Cajun—
A World of Difference!?

Once and for all, the term "Creole" is not synonymous with the term "Cajun." Yes, they both pertain to Louisiana. Yes, they both are related to the development of Louisiana history. But when we visited Boston even the elite on Harvard Yard asked, "So you're from New Orleans—are you a Cajun?" Really! Do Graham or Taylor sound like Cajun names? How about Creole names? Taylor and Graham are about as WASP as one can get (besides, as we drank wine at Harvard, no one heard us asking if anyone was a descendant of an old, Tory, traitor family).

Although there remains some argument about the derivation of the word "Creole," defining "Cajun" draws little fanfare or controversy. Originally dubbed "Cajuns" by early American settlers in Louisiana, they were actually Acadians who had been forcibly "resettled" from Canada to south Louisiana. Most Cajuns settled in rural Louisiana along the many bayous that would provide food, occupations, and shelter. Today the Cajun regional dialect can still be traced to its roots in provincial France. For a taste of this culture, drive southwest of New Orleans to places named Chauvin, Lafourche, Dulac, Abbeville, or Thibodaux. Take along a map and a passport.

Now, Creole generally refers to old New Orleans before the Americans arrived. Primarily the colonial French families and, later, the Spanish colonials were the original Creoles. However, generally speaking, Creoles were those families who settled before the Louisiana Purchase in 1803. This was before the great American influx. Creole family names are still carried on in New Orleans: Nunez, Doucet, Livaudais, and Villere, to name a few.

But enough history. Let's be practical. When you think of Cajun, picture rural, bayou country in south Louisiana and roughly west of the Mississippi River. This does not include New Orleans.

Traditional Cajun foods tend to take advantage of available vegetables (bell peppers, onions, celery, etc.), wildlife, and seafood, and accent local seasonings (garlic and cayenne pepper in particular), and, of course, the ever-present rice that is found in countless Cajun dishes (jambalaya, étouffée, boudin, etc.). Cajun food is highly seasoned, but not necessarily hot as hell.

Creole, on the other hand, should be associated with New Orleans. It is basically an urban term now, but was applicable to anyone settling before the Americans and Cajuns arrived. Creole foods are richer in taste than their Cajun counterparts. Many Creole dishes call for sauces, and rice is used less. Also, Creole food is not as hearty nor as highly seasoned as Cajun food. Many people assume Creole food is more sophisticated than Cajun food because the titles of many dishes are always capitalized (Oysters Bienville, Trout Meuniere, etc.).

There are numerous exceptions to what we have just purported regarding the cuisine of the area. As a matter of fact, the exceptions may negate the definitions. It's all one gastronomical grey area anyway. So consider all this only as a rule of thumb, as the overlaps are immense and, frankly, academic. (But if you desire a delightful examination of Cajun and Creole foods, we suggest you read *La Cuisine Cajun*, by Jude W. Theriot, and *La Bouche Creole*, by Leon E. Soniat, Jr., both published by Pelican.)

Chefs, food critics, and connoisseurs alike will argue the merits of the aforementioned claims concerning the differences in Creole and Cajun foods. While they debate, we're going to lay waste to a pot of seafood gumbo with French bread. Or is it gumbo with a capital *G*? Vive la difference and pass the filé.

The Authors

ALAN GRAHAM, a descendent of the second oldest clan in Scotland, is a native New Orleanian and the conceptual creator of this book. He has been a waiter, bartender, restaurant manager, teacher, high-school principal, corporate consultant, and spent four years at Tulane heading a societal-change project. As its executive director, Alan created what was once this state's modern-day education reform movement, the Louisiana Alliance for Education Reform.

Alan is the proud father of a rather large litter of children, Ross, Brittany, Chelsea, and Tess, all named for places in Europe except for Tess (of the D'Urbervilles).

JAMES TAYLOR, in an effort to avoid being confused with that other guy who sings, prefers the simple appellation of Jim. In past incarnations he has been a teacher, writer, and filmmaker. He is now a New Orleans attorney.

Since the mid-seventies Jim has been married to Dottie Estes, and during the eighties they became the parents of Jameson and Mallory. The demands of career and family have curtailed the night life somewhat as they head into the turn of the century, but even so, they continue to be observers of the current trends and established traditions that make New Orleans the most exotic city in the Western Hemisphere.